The Mystic Core

SPIRITUALITY IN THE AGE OF MATERIALISM

The Mystic Core

SPIRITUALITY IN THE AGE OF MATERIALISM

RON FROST

SacraSage

First Edition: March 2022
Print ISBN 978-1-948609-59-3
Ebook ISBN 978-1-948609-60-9
Printed in the United States of America

———————————————————————————

Library of Congress Cataloguing-in-Publication Data
The Mystic Core: Spirituality in the Age of Materialism / Ron Frost

To Nancy Huszagh and all the others

who kept the retreat center at Söpa Chöling running

as one of the premier retreat centers in North America

Contents

How this book came to be

The heavily falling snow imparted a milky glow to the night sky, allowing me to find my way without a light to where I could watch the woods fill up with snow.

I stood mid-calf in the snow watching the fat fluffy flakes spinning and swirling in the windless night and listening to the subtle pish-pish as they fell into the surrounding woods.

A thought flitted into my mind that each of the lazily falling flakes was different, and that an infinite number of shapes were drifting around me.

Suddenly, that sense of the infinite exploded and enveloped my mind. The world about me seemed to turn inside out, and I found myself immersed in a powerful white light.

The experience lasted for a few seconds at most, and when the light disappeared and the falling snow reappeared, I found myself kneeling in the snow.

I was 16 when this happened, and I lived in Cedar Grove, New Jersey. At the time, in the early 1960s, Cedar Grove was near the western margin of the suburbs of New York City. The subdivisions that were sprouting up in the area were still surrounded by significant amounts of undeveloped land, where I spent my leisure time. I had been raised in a staunchly atheist family. My father never lost an opportunity to rave about the horrors of the Inquisition and the insidious way that religion, Christianity in particular, has fought so hard to impede the progress of humanity. Consequently, I had no context in which to put the experience that I had had in the snow. I told no one about it afterwards, partially because I could not describe it. The description that I have written above hardly gives justice to the sense of awe and wonder the event carried with it, nor does it convey the certainty that I had experienced something special. Even if I could have put it into words that were more precise than those above, I had the deep suspicion that no one would believe me. However, just because I didn't talk about it, the effects of the experience did not go away. It had dramatically shown me that there was more to reality than the physical world, an insight that took up residence deep in my psyche.

My father was a chemist and regularly entertained me with the wonders of chemistry, spectacular demonstrations that today would be considered completely unsafe, if not illegal. I particularly remember the night when he lit a piece of magnesium metal in our front yard. It illuminated the whole street and totally impressed me and the whole community of children who had gathered to see the demonstration. For better or worse, I entered college with the feeling that science was an exciting field of study and that education was designed to give me tools to make a living in life. I decided to major in geology because it combined my interest in science with my love of the out-of-doors. I labored through undergraduate and graduate school, relishing my courses in geology and the opportunity they gave me to understand how the earth worked and how mountains formed. Behind the scenes, though, I found myself reading a broad array of books about spirituality. I read Thoreau and the Transcendentalists in high school, and in college I began to attack various books on Eastern Religions, which were just beginning to appear in the West at that time.

I earned my Ph.D. from the University of Washington in 1973 and after years of temporary employment, ended up in 1978 with my dream job, Assistant Professor of Geology at the University of Wyoming, a state whose mountains beckoned to me. The mountains expose some of the oldest rocks in the world and, at that time, they were very little studied. I threw myself into my new job with a relish and, with the help of colleagues at the University of Wyoming, began slowly unraveling the complex history that the rocks recorded; a history that goes back nearly four billion years.

In the fall of 1983, soon after getting tenure, I saw a notice on campus advertising a weekend program on the introduction to Buddhist meditation. For years, I had read about Eastern Religions and this program was something I had been looking for. Before the weekend was over, I knew that I had found my spiritual path. I was thrilled to have stumbled into a religion that, like science, was empirical. I was instructed to simply sit and follow the meditation instructions and to see what happened. Here was a spiritual practice that did not require any previous beliefs, and I embraced it with gusto.

I didn't know at the time, but I was about to be caught up in a wave of realization that was rippling out from one of the greatest humanitarian disasters of the 20th century. In 1950, China occupied Tibet under the ruse of liberating the people from a feudal government. Originally, the Chinese governed Tibet as an autonomous region, and for nine years, the Tibetan government under the Dalai Lama struggled to maintain some degree of autonomy. Finally, in 1959, the Tibetan people revolted under the Chinese rule and China acted quickly to crush the revolt. More than 100,000 of the elite of Tibetan society escaped across the Himalayan Mountains to India. The Chinese crackdown involved a reign of terror, during which thousands of Tibetans died, the major Tibetan monasteries were leveled, and countless Buddhist texts, images, and relics were burnt.

Among the thousands of people who were driven from Tibet by the Chinese invasion were dozens of Rinpoches. In Tibetan Buddhism, the word Rinpoche, which is translated as "precious one", describes a person who is considered a reincarnated lama. Rinpoches are recognized when they are very young and undergo extensive training in the techniques and liturgies of Tibetan Buddhism. Thus, though most of the buildings, artwork, and books of Tibetan Buddhism had been destroyed by the Chinese, the heart of the Buddhist teachings escaped within the minds of the Rinpoches and other Buddhist monks who flocked into India. The Chinese certainly had no idea that their attempt to snuff out Buddhism in Tibet would spread Tibetan Buddhism to the rest of the world. Fifty years after the Chinese holocaust, Tibetan Buddhism had become a world-wide religion with centers in almost every Western and Asian city.

Among the many Rinpoches driven out of Tibet by the Chinese holocaust were three young men who would have a profound impact on Buddhism in the West, Tenzin Gyatso (who was 24 at the time), Khenchen Thrangu (who was 29), and Chögyam Trungpa (who was 20). Tenzin Gyatso, the 14th Dalai Lama, was not only a highly trained lama, he was also the head of the Tibetan government. Many people are familiar with the story of his attempts to accommodate the Chinese and his ultimate exile from Tibet, as told in Martin Scorsese's movie *Kundun*. When he entered India after fleeing Tibet, the Dalai Lama was a penniless refugee, the unknown deposed leader of a remote country on the roof of Asia. Upon his arrival in India, he helped establish a home for exiled Tibetans in Dharamshala, India. Over the following decades, through the power of his personality, he kept the plight of Tibet in the mind of the world. His efforts to gain Tibetan freedom through peaceful means won him the Nobel Peace Prize in 1989. He continues to travel the world and to teach Buddhism and is considered one of the most admired men in the world.

Khenchen Thrangu Rinpoche and Chögyam Trungpa Rinpoche were both major figures in the Kagyü school of Tibetan Buddhism, but each followed a distinctly different path after leaving Tibet. Thrangu Rinpoche put his efforts into maintaining and building traditional Buddhist facilities, first in the Himalaya region, then throughout Asia, and finally in North America and Europe. He has become one of the most important sources of Buddhist teachings in the Tibetan community and has published nearly 50 books on the esoteric details of Tibetan Buddhism.

Trungpa Rinpoche learned English, studied comparative religion at Oxford, renounced his monastic vows, married, and migrated to America in 1970, where he ended up in Boulder, Colorado, which at the time had a thriving counter-culture. Trungpa Rinpoche quickly drew a cadre of devoted students who learned Buddhist meditation from him and who began teaching it around the region. It was one of his senior students who taught the program I attended in Laramie in 1983. With a group of students who had learned Tibetan, Trungpa established The Nalanda Translation Committee, and they began the arduous job of translating with him the major texts of the Kagyü tradition into English. Once the texts were translated, Trungpa began teaching students the advanced practices of Tibetan Buddhism, practices that previously had been restricted to monks cloistered in monasteries in Tibet. In 1983, he established Gampo Abbey, a Kagyü monastery, in Cape Breton, Nova Scotia and, since he was no longer an ordained monk, he asked Thrangu Rinpoche to be the abbot of the monastery. Trungpa Rinpoche moved the headquarters of his organization to Halifax, Nova Scotia in 1986; he died of heart failure there the following year. His influence in transmitting Buddhism to the West is unparalleled. He and his students developed Buddhist centers throughout the U.S., Canada, and Europe. He is the author of 50 books that are designed to introduce Western students to all aspects of Tibetan Buddhism; many of those books were published after his death from transcripts of talks he had given.

For more than 30 years after joining the faculty at the University of Wyoming, I climbed the academic ladder; wandering the mountains of Wyoming and studying the rocks that I found there. I also made investigations on rocks elsewhere in the world, including the Alps, Greenland, Canada, Australia, and the ocean floor off the Mid-Atlantic Ridge. All the while, whenever opportunity presented itself, I deepened my Buddhist practice by taking many weekend (or longer) retreats.

One morning in the year 2000, I awoke with the quixotic idea to comment on the great debate between geologists and Creationists on the origin of the Earth. It took me years to write the book *On Science and Religion. Where Both Sides Go Wrong On The Great Evolution Debate.* In that book I noted that, although the errors of the Young Earth Christian Fundamentalists are obvious, in that they take the myths of the Bible as being absolute fact, however, I noted that the materialistic scientists are also wrong in contending that there is no spiritual aspect to life. The book appeared in 2010 and the act of writing it gave me important insights into contemporary disputes between science and religion, especially fundamentalist Christianity.

One of the insights I derived from writing that book was the realization that the gulf between science and religion (or at least the mystical aspect of religion) was much broader than is usually recognized. Mystics of all religions maintain that the true mystical view of reality is that there is no difference between you and your experience. In other words, for the mystic there is no difference between the objective and subjective world. In the Hindu and Buddhist view, the objective world is *maya*—an illusion. The difference between this view and that of a scientist, particularly that of a geologist, cannot be more extreme. For scientists, the outside world exists, is solid, and the best way to dissect it is through scientific investigation.

I have been very successful as a scientist. I have no doubt that there is an outside world and that science does a fairly good job of describing it. Not only that, scientific advances in understanding the world, for extracting resources, understanding the environment, and solving medical problems is absolutely crucial for the health of our modern economy. However, I am also convinced that the mystical experience exists, that it is beyond description, and that our society needs to root itself in the mystical experience if people are to develop themselves to the greatest extent possible.

The problem is that the scientific and mystical views of reality seem to be inherently contradictory. How was I to find a way to bridge the huge gulf between them? I eventually concluded that the only way I could do this was for me to become a mystic myself. To do this, I decided to enroll in the Three-Year Retreat, which is perhaps the most intense mystical practice available. The Three-Year Retreat is the ultimate training in Tibetan Buddhism. For hundreds of years, the various sects of Buddhism in Tibet educated their upcoming students on a one-to-one basis with senior teachers. In the seventeenth century, the sects introduced the Three-Year Retreat, an intense meditative program during which the students would be introduced to all the practices of the particular sect of Buddhism with which they were involved. In Tibet, the students who participated in the retreats were mostly in their late teens or twenties and when they were finished, they generally became teachers themselves.

The first Three-Year Retreat in the West was held in 1972-1975 in France under Kalu Rinpoche. In the 1990s, students of Trungpa Rinpoche began pushing for a three-year retreat of their own. They raised money to construct a retreat center at Gampo Abbey, which was given the name Söpa Chöling—which means roughly "place of patient practice of the Dharma". Thrangu Rinpoche became the head of the retreat; he organized the curriculum and set the Nalanda Translation Committee to work translating the various liturgies that were to be used in the retreat. In 1996, the building at Söpa Chöling was complete, the texts needed for the first year had been translated, and the first year of the first retreat began.

The retreat at Söpa Chöling was unique. It was the only Three-Year Retreat in the world that was conducted in English. In addition, it was conducted over a 5-year period, with three years of retreat interspersed with two years back in society. It was also located in a spectacular site. The retreat center was perched on a 200-foot-high cliff above the Gulf of St. Laurence, which afforded a spectacular view of the Gulf. In the summer and early fall, we were treated to views of the array of sea life in the North Atlantic, including whales, seals, and abundant white diving birds, the Northern Gannets. In the winter, the retreat center provided views of the constantly changing sea ice in the Gulf.

The Söpa Chöling retreat required a lot of prerequisites—mostly in the form of meditation programs—and I finally finished all of them in 2010. I enrolled in the retreat that began in 2012 as part of the seventh group to do the retreat. I was on retreat during the years of 2012-2013, 2014-2015, and 2016-2017; during those years, I took temporary ordination as a monk. Each person on retreat was assigned a room that measured 8 feet x 12 feet; most of the rooms afforded a sweeping view of the gulf. The room was outfitted with a shrine, a large meditation box, and no bed. You had to either sleep in the box, which I managed to do for most of the retreat, or sleep on a foam pad that could be stored away during the day. Each day would begin by a wake-up gong at 5:00 AM and we would meditate until 9:30 at night. During the three years we would engage in various meditative practices; usually we would practice around 11 hours a day.

This book is a result of the insights I gained during the retreat. Participants of the retreat commonly have many insights as a result of the long time spent in meditation. Traditionally, it is deemed poor form in the Tibetan community to talk about your meditative insights. It is considered a very unsubtle form of bragging and, more importantly, teachers think that when you share an insight with others, you lose the impact that it has on your mind. Unfortunately, I found that when writing this book, I had to selectively violate this rule. It is fine to hold all of your experiences secret when you are immersed in a religious society, where the nature of the religious experience is understood. However, when writing for materialists, who not only dispute the existence of these experiences, but who commonly belittle those who describe having them, I found that it was important for me to discuss some of these experiences. It is an effort, perhaps in vain, to convince the materialists that these experiences do exist and that they are incredibly valuable.

Although this was a strict meditative retreat, and not one where I should spend my time writing, I could not keep the thoughts of this book from my mind. I had read all the books by atheists and materialists while working on my book on evolution and was well aware of their arguments. Beginning in the middle of the second year of retreat, ideas about how to answer the arguments of the atheists would intrude into my dreams and idle thoughts. The book mostly wrote itself in my mind during the third year of the retreat—at least I thought it did. However, after returning to Laramie from the retreat in the fall of 2017, when I finally sat down to put it "on paper" (i.e. into my computer), I found that the text that had written itself in my mind was full of holes that I had to fill in laboriously. It took until early 2020 for me to complete the first draft.

Acknowledgments

This work would never have seen the light of day without assistance from many friends and acquaintances. Foremost among these are Catie Ballard, who is a stalwart of the Unitarian Church, and Reverend Dr. Sally Palmer from the United Church of Christ. Sal and Catie read over the early versions of the text and gave me many suggestions about how I could expand my book to include Christian spirituality in addition to the Buddhist spirituality upon which it was originally based. I would also like to thank Rabbi Rami Shapiro, who patiently helped me understand Jewish mysticism, especially as manifested in the Jewish Renewal Movement. Like the advice from Sally Palmer and Catie Ballard, Rabbi Shapiro's advice strongly enhanced the interspiritual nature of the book.

I would also like to thank all the participants of the 2021 Contemplative Camp at La Foret Retreat Center in Colorado. We used a Xerox copy of this book as a reading for this camp and discussion with all the participants helped me focus the arguments I have used in the book. I particularly wish to thank Barbara Maxwell from this camp, who carefully proofread the rough draft for the manuscript and corrected many little mistakes that were hiding therein.

CHAPTER 1

Two Views of Reality

INTRODUCTION

What is the meaning of life? Are we and all other creatures in the world simply mechanical beings, whose only meaning lies within the genes we carry, whose actions are blindly learned responses to stimuli and whose thoughts are merely chemical reactions in our brains? Is the value of people found only in the stuff that they own? What happens at the end of the rat-race? Does the light simply turn off? If so, why not enjoy whatever joys we can find, regardless of the effect it has on others?

An answer of "yes" to most of these profound questions carries with it a depressing implication that life is flat and superficial.

Isn't there something more to life than this continual interplay of impulse and reaction? Isn't there something more to existence than simply existing? Isn't there some insight we can gain that allows us to bear with equanimity the problems and disappointments we encounter in life? Can that insight help us to see others, not as competitors, but as beings who are caught in the same struggles as we are?

These questions have troubled humans ever since we developed the ability to communicate. This existential pondering appears in the earliest texts written more than 3000 years ago. These questions have become even more significant over the past centuries in Western society, where the growth of scientific knowledge accompanied by the development of prolific technology has been balanced with a simultaneous growth of a materialistic view of life. Materialism is characterized by a highly logical view of reality; a process that is often called linear thinking.

Before getting too far into the discussion of materialism, it is beholden upon me to define terms that I will use in this book. *Materialism* is the metaphysical theory that nothing exists outside of the physical realm. One could simply characterize this by the statement: "If you cannot see it or measure it, then it doesn't exist". In some respects, materialism is synonymous with *atheism*, which maintains that there is no God or spiritual dimension beyond the physical world. In the early 21st century, a type of atheism known as *neoatheism* arose that uses materialist and scientific arguments to decry religion in all forms[1]. Some religions, however, foremost among them Buddhism, also contend that there is no God; strictly speaking, they are atheistic. Buddhism often refers to itself as a *non-theistic* religion, to make it evident that it accepts the existence of a spiritual dimension, even if it doesn't endow it with any personal attributes.

In this book I will use the terms materialism and atheism rather interchangeably, although in this context the atheism I will be referring to will be specifically the concepts and arguments of neoatheism. I will use the term "materialism" when considering the view that only the physical world exists. I will use "atheism" when I am considering contentions that specifically argue against religions or the existence of a spiritual dimension.

The growth of materialism in our society has had a strong negative effect on our society's understanding of religion. Rational, linear thinking became the dominant way of looking at the world in the late 18th and early 19th centuries. In response to the success that rational thought had to unraveling the mysteries of the physical world, in the late 19th century, a movement arose that advocated the application of linear thinking to the study of religious scriptures. This resulted in the formation of fundamentalist religious sects that relied upon belief in a literal interpretation of the scriptures[2]. Fundamentalists tend to look back to a simpler time when society had firmly established societal, gender, and religious rules. As a result, fundamentalism tends to affirm staunchly conservative views of how society should be organized and considers modern societies to be inherently sinful or evil.

The socially conservative view of the fundamentalists makes it appear that religion is out of touch with modern cultural trends.

This, coupled with the atheistic world-view of our material-istic society, which is disdainful of religion, has put traditional religion under stress and has caused it to become increasingly marginalized. Between 2007 and 2019, the percentage of Americans that considered themselves Christian had decreased from 78% to 65% while the percentage who adhered to no religion (the "nones") had increased from 16% to 25%[3]. Rabbi Rami Shapiro points out that the term "nones" has a distinctly negative connotation. Generally, these people are not atheists, but they are searching for spiritual values outside of traditional religion. As a result, Shapiro refers to them as *spiritual independents*[4].

The data also shows a huge generational gap in religious affil-iation. Of those Americans who were born between 1928 and 1945, 84% consider themselves Christian, as do 76% of Baby Boomers. In contrast, only 49% of Millennials consider them-selves Christian. Nearly the same proportion of Millennials ~ 40% consider themselves "nones" and ~10% of them adhere to other religions[5]. It is in this growing spiritual turmoil that this existential question about the meaning of life must be addressed again.

The discussion above hints at this question: "What is the nature of mind[6]?" We are all aware of the interior dialogue that dominates our thoughts in a seemingly endless manner. What is the cause of this mental chatter? This question is one of the important subjects of this book. According to the materialist view, consciousness is an epiphenomenon that somehow arises from electrical or chemical reactions in the brain. Religious people maintain that there are aspects of mind that arise, not from matter, but from some external source. This source is spiritual, which is an important term that needs to be defined here.

The word "spirit" comes from the Latin word *"spiritus"*, which means "breath". In Hebrew, the connotations are the same: the word *"ruah"* means "spirit", but also "wind" and "breath". These definitions carry the implication that spirit is something immaterial from outside our body that animates us. Just as breath animates the body, spirit animates the mind. To Christians, and people of many other religions, the term "spirit" refers to God. To Buddhists, the spiritual dimension is real, although ascribing personal attributes to God is not part of our practice. Although my spiritual life is not built around a belief in God, this does not mean that I am an atheist. If someone were to ask me if I, as a Buddhist, believe in God, I would answer: "Sure, God is the spring from which my consciousness sprouts."

All the world's religions maintain that spirit is both immanent and transcendent. This means that the spiritual dimension manifests itself both within a person and outside of a person. The immanent aspect of spirituality produces a person's personality, consciousness, and emotions. The transcendent aspect of spirituality is the sense one has that there is something greater to reality than oneself. It can manifest as a sense of awe when one encounters the expanses of nature, be it in the complexities of the microbiological world, the wildness of the wilderness, or the vastness of space. Transcendence can also manifest in one's mind when one experiences creativity, intuition, or premonition, experiences where thoughts, concepts, or insights appear spontaneously within one's mind. For me, I get a great feeling of transcendence from the act of creativity. When I sit down to write something, I usually have an idea of what I want to get across, but commonly, afterwards, when I read over what I have written, I am stunned. I would often say to myself, "Wow, this is awesome! Where did it come from?" I have often told people that I did not write this book; it wrote itself through me. What did the writing is a complete mystery; which is the nature of transcendent spirituality. To materialists, of course, the feelings of immanence and transcendence described by spiritual folks simply do not register. To them, all these feelings are simply chemical reactions in the brain and, therefore, it is clearly foolish to construct a world-view upon them.

TWO VIEWS OF REALITY

The conflict between the world-view of materialism and that of spiritual people reflects a dispute on the nature of reality that extends back to the very beginnings of Western philosophy. The differences in these worldviews are summarized in Figure I and will be discussed in detail in the rest of the chapter.

In the materialist view (Fig. IA) the most important thing in the universe is matter, living beings are simply another type of matter and consciousness is present only in a tiny proportion of living beings, perhaps only in humans. In the spiritual view (Fig. IB) the most important thing in the universe is consciousness, which permeates and energizes all life. Matter, although it makes up most of the volume of the universe, is not nearly as important.

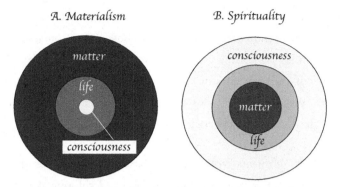

Figure 1. *Two views of reality. A. In materialism, matter is the most important thing in the universe and life is mostly matter. Consciousness is limited to a few evolved animals. B. In spirituality, consciousness is the most important thing in the universe; it may well extend to all life. Matter is simply the substrate upon which all this occurs. Modified from Frost (2010).*

MATERIALISM. As noted above, materialism affirms that physical substances are the only components in the universe. Over the past four centuries, as science came to explain more and more of the phenomenal world, materialism has grown to be the major philosophic view of Western society. Materialists contend that the world is entirely produced by physical processes. Key to this philosophy is the concept that reality arises from elementary particles through the process of emergence. The theory of emergence states that, as a system becomes more complex, evolving from sub-atomic particles, to elements, to compounds, new properties arise that were not present in the simpler systems.

For example, elements are constructed from elementary particles—electrons, protons and neutrons[7]. Each electron, proton and neutron in the universe is identical to every other electron, proton, and neutron. These elementary particles combine to form elements. Each element has distinct properties, such as mass, valance, melting point, that are dependent on the number and configuration of electrons that it contains (of course, each electron is balanced by a proton that lies within the nucleus)[8]. None of the properties of the elements are present in the electrons, protons, or neutrons themselves; they emerge from the way these elementary particles have coalesced.

Similarly, elements combine in various ways to produce compounds. For example, sodium (Na) and chlorine (Cl) are both elements that can cause grievous harm or death if ingested. When they react together, they form NaCl, a compound called salt, which is vital for life. Salt also contains emergent properties, such as a cubic shape, solubility in water and a salty taste, which are not present in the original elements. Chemists recognize more than 100 elements, most of which are quite rare, and these may be combined to form a bewildering number of compounds, each of which has distinctive emergent chemical properties.

Materialists contend that, similar to the way that salty taste is an emergent property of salt, life and consciousness are also emergent properties of matter. They point out that living beings are composed of organic compounds, which are composed of carbon, oxygen, hydrogen, nitrogen, and a smattering of minor elements such as sulfur and phosphorous. According to materialists, when organic compounds are arranged in the proper way, another emergent property, known as life, arises. Furthermore, they believe that, as living beings evolved, their neurological systems became more complex. In the materialist view, when the neurologic makeup of life becomes sufficiently complex, yet another emergent property appears—consciousness. This is the background inherent in the following statement (the italics were part of the original text):

> The prevailing wisdom, variously expressed and argued for, is *materialism:* there is only one sort of stuff, namely *matter*—the physical stuff of physics, chemistry, physiology—and the mind is somehow nothing but a physical phenomenon. In short, the mind is the brain. According to materialists, we can (in principle!) account for every mental phenomenon using the same physical principles, laws and raw materials that suffice to explain radioactivity, continental drift, photosynthesis, reproduction, nutrition, and growth[9].

In addition to viewing mental phenomena as mere chemical reactions, materialists also consider that humans and all other creatures are simply physical beings who are responding to instinctive needs or selfish desires. To materialists, there is no need to call upon a spiritual dimension to life; all one needs to describe our perception of reality is to understand the biochemical processes that occur within our cells.

SPIRITUALITY. Spirituality is the philosophical notion that an immaterial reality exists. A suite of terms exists describing the relation between the physical and spiritual dimensions[10], but to reduce confusion, I will combine them all into a single term "spirituality". When I use the term, it implies that there is a spiritual realm that coexists with and permeates the physical realm. It is important to note that the physical dimension postulated here is similar to the physical dimension postulated by materialists.

As is commonly expressed by religions, reality consists of two aspects—relative reality, which is manifested by the physical world around us, and ultimate or absolute reality, which is the spiritual dimension that exists within and beyond the realms of relative reality. Rabbi Rami Shapiro has a very poetic way of expressing these differences:

> Imagine that you are a wave in a vast shoreless sea. Imagine further that you realize that you and all the other waves of this sea are nothing other than the sea waving, extending itself in time and space. You are still you—a wave–and yet so much more than you—the sea itself. Knowing yourself as the wave is knowing the relative world, the world of seemingly separate beings. Knowing yourself as the sea is knowing the absolute world, the world of One who is all these seemingly separate waves. But there is still another level of knowing—the unlabeled knowing that knows both sea and wave, both the absolute and relative[11].

According to this understanding, materialists have a myopic, limited view of reality; they are concerned only with the waves, whereas spiritual people recognize that both the waves and the sea are part of the same reality. Mystics try to move one step further and to understand the unlabeled knowing that understands the interplay of the relative and absolute.

The recognition that a spiritual dimension exists leads to an individual's endeavor to understand it. This produces the following definition of spirituality:

> The term spirituality refers to an individual's solitary search for and discovery of the absolute or the divine. It involves a direct mystical experience of God...
>
> Spirituality carries with it a conviction that the transcendent is real, and it requires some sort of spiritual practice that acts as a catalyst for inner change and growth[12].

Spirituality is core to most religions. Consider, for example, the quote from the Dalai Lama:

> Finally, then when considering the interrelationship between mind, body and the environment at the subtle level, we know that material things are composed of cells, atoms and particles and that consciousness is composed of moments. That is to say that mind and matter have distinctly different natures and therefore have different substantial causes[13].

Of course, there might be a dispute between individual religions over how to interpret the spiritual, but the existence of a spiritual dimension is definitely the root of religion.

Although spirituality may be the root of all religions, it doesn't mean that the words "religion" and "spirituality" are synonyms. Religions are human institutions that have been designed to provide practitioners with access to spirituality. There are differences between the symbols, rituals, and doctrine that individual religions use to attain this goal and this leads to subtle differences between the connotations inherent in the terms "religion" and "spirituality", as noted in the quote below (italics come from the original quote):

> Being *religious* connotes belonging to and practicing a religious tradition. Being *spiritual* suggests a personal commitment to a process of inner development that engages us in our totality. Religion is, of course, one way that people are spiritual.... Still, not every religious person is spiritual (although they ought to be!), and not every spiritual person is religious[14].

Religious practitioners consider that life and consciousness are part of a spiritual dimension that permeates the physical dimension They consider that the major problem with the materialists' theory that life and consciousness are emergent properties is that these emergent properties are very different from the other emergent properties that scientists deal with. Chemists easily use the configuration of the electrons within an atom of an element to explain how the emergent properties of that element originate. Similarly, they can explain the emergent properties of chemical compounds based upon the types and strengths of chemical bonds between the atoms in those compounds. In contrast, science does a very poor job of explaining how life could arise as an emergent property from a mixture of organic chemicals. Similarly, it does a poor job of explaining how consciousness could arise from interactions of neurons in the brain.

To those who recognize a spiritual dimension to life, consciousness, and the life around us are much more wondrous than the flat world presented by materialists. We humans are so used to living in a world teeming with life that we seldom take a moment to realize how special life is. Living beings have two properties that are distinctive from non-living matter. First, life is able to reproduce, which means that individual creatures are able to produce copies of themselves. Secondly, creatures have a metabolism, which means that they are able to produce complex hydrocarbons, such as proteins and sugars, from simple compounds such as carbon dioxide (CO_2) and water (H_2O). These distinctive features mean that life is anti-entropic—i.e. that it operates against entropy.

Entropy is the chemical function that describes how any system left on its own will evolve into the most simple and random state possible. We all know this intuitively. We know that our hot coffee will cool if we let it sit around for a while, whereas our cold beer will get warmer. Likewise, if we hang our newly washed sheets out on a clothesline on a sunny day, they will spontaneously dry. All these processes are the manifestations of entropy. As long as a creature is alive, it seems immune to entropy. Throughout its life, a creature will work against entropy by taking simple compounds, such as CO_2 and H_2O and combining them into complex hydrocarbons that are incorporated into the creature's body so it can grow and survive. As soon as the creature dies, however, its immunity to entropy disappears. The process of entropy takes over, and the body begins to decay. During this process, the hydrocarbons of the creature's body, which were amassed when the creature was alive, react with oxygen in the atmosphere to produce the simple compounds of CO_2 and H_2O. Thus, entropy, which was kept at bay while the animal was alive, finally takes over when the animal dies and it works to reduce the animal's body to its chemical constituents.

There is something special about life that allows it to run against entropy. One can always decrease entropy by adding energy to the system. For example, one can make one's cold coffee hot again by warming it up in the microwave oven. Life works against entropy through metabolism. The approach that life takes toward metabolism can be broadly subdivided into two classes: *autotrophic* and *heterotrophic*. Autotrophs (a word that means "self-nutrition") make their own food from sunlight, as in photoautotrophs, or from chemical reactions in rocks or soil, as in chemoautotrophs. All autotrophs are plants. Heterotrophs (a word that means "other-nutrition") obtain their energy from eating autotrophs.

The key question is, what is the process driving metabolism that allows life to operate and that, once it disappears, that permits decay to set in? Even a four-year-old can tell that there is a distinct difference between a squirrel scurrying across the street and the same squirrel moments later after it has been run over by a car. Many spiritual people contend that the difference is a spiritual energy, which philosophers such as Henri

Bergson (1859-1941) describe as the "vital force". According to Bergson, the vital force is also the driving force for creativity, and it appears in our minds as consciousness. Materialists are totally dismissive of the concept of vitalism:

> To materialists the vitality of life is nothing other than an emergent property that appears once a certain critical state of complexity has been reached. This emergent property drives the metabolism of an organism and continues to do so until the parts of the organism begin to wear out, at which point the organism dies. The arguments materialists make against vitalism are not particularly persuasive... simply dropping the name "vital force" and calling it some unspecified "emergent property" doesn't make the mystery of life go away, although it does, apparently give materialists an excuse to ignore it[15].

A major problem with the argument materialists make against the existence of a vital force is that there is ample empirical evidence in Asian societies that a vital force exists, where it is called *qi* or *chi* (in Chinese), *prana* (in Sanskrit) and *lung* (in Tibetan). These societies have various techniques, for example meditation, acupuncture, yoga, tai chi, and karate, to access this energy and to use it to induce healing and to provide power and vitality.

A key question, and one of the most important themes in this book, is: *what is the nature of our consciousness?* As noted above, materialists maintain that consciousness appears when creatures develop a brain that is complex enough so that interactions between many synapses produce the emergent property of consciousness. Mystics, on the other hand, believe that consciousness comes from outside the body. It is hard to establish which model is correct because it is very difficult to determine if a creature, even a human, is conscious. This problem was brought home to me dramatically one day when I had a bicycle accident while on sabbatical in Canberra. I have no idea what caused the accident; it gave me a classic case of retrograde amnesia. I was bicycling toward the Australian National University on a sunny summer day. The last thing I remember was bicycling along the sidewalk a mile from the northwest entrance to the university. Next, I found myself on the ground, while a group of people had gathered around and were talking to me and to each other.

"Hold still, mate," one voice said, "the ambulance is on the way." The speaker did not need to worry; I couldn't move a muscle. I couldn't even open my eyes.

"Look at that arm," another voice said. "I am sure the elbow is dislocated." In response to this comment, I ran my attention down both arms but could not find pain in either one. It turns out that my left elbow wasn't dislocated; the injury was simply a classic case of road rash. I passed out after that but came aware again as the ambulance crew were loading me on a backboard. They did a very smooth job of transferring me to the board.

"Good job, fellows." I said to myself, "If you were in one of my tests, I would surely pass you." I am on Ski Patrol in our local ski area and for many years I had taught the advanced first aid to the candidates who wanted to become ski patrollers. Many times, I had been the "patient" that candidates had to move onto a backboard, and I knew how tricky the maneuver can be. The thought that I was mentally comparing the first aid abilities of the professional Canberra ambulance crew with my amateur Ski Patrol students was ridiculous and it would have made me laugh—had I been able to.

When I took Ski Patrol first aid in the early 90s we were taught to assess a patient's mental status, or *level of consciousness,* as it was called at the time, by determining if the patient could respond to verbal commands, if they could only respond to pain, such as a pinch on the ear, or could not respond at all. I had been unconscious when the ambulance first arrived and one of the EMTs assessed my mental abilities. However, even if I had been experiencing one of my momentary periods of lucidity that followed the accident, I would have been able to hear the EMT talking to me but I would not have been able to respond to her voice or the pinch she would have given me (even if I could have felt it). Over the years, the medical community came to realize that there is simply no way for a doctor (or a nurse or an EMT) can determine whether a person who does not respond to a voice or to a gentle pinch is conscious or not. As a result of that, sometime in the late 1990s, the medical community dropped the term *"level of consciousness"* and replaced it with *"level of responsiveness"* to emphasize that a person could be conscious but unresponsive, as I was on the tarmac at ANU.

If it is difficult to determine if humans are conscious, then it is much more difficult to determine whether animals are conscious and how far down the chain of life consciousness goes. The only evidence we have to infer whether animals are conscious is their behavior. Those materialists who contend that humans are the only conscious animal, clearly never had a dog. For years, I had a pit bull-cross named "Jackie". Usually, when I came home from work, she would greet me enthusiastically, ready for her afternoon walk. Sometimes, however, when I came home, I would find her lying on the floor with her head between her front paws, looking mournfully at me. Whenever I saw this, I knew that Jackie had gotten into the garbage in the kitchen. When this happened, I would clean up the kitchen, give her a ritual dressing down, and then we would head out for our walk. Jackie obviously knew that the garbage was off limits, but sometimes the smell it carried was too tempting. When that happened, though, she knew she had misbehaved and showed some sign of remorse. That behavior, being able to understand the consequences of one's actions, surely is an indication of consciousness.

One of the most charming things about our retreat at Söpa Chöling was the behavior of the chickadees. Over years, the monastics at Gampo Abbey had trained the resident Black-Capped Chickadees to eat out of their hands. The Boreal Chickadees were not willing to participate in the game, although frequently they would watch the proceedings from a nearby tree. The chickadees did not bother to demonstrate their training during the summer and autumn when there was plenty of other food around, but when winter came, the birds regularly beseeched us for food whenever we were outside. On snowy days in the winter, I would go outside to shovel snow during the half hour of free time that we had between morning meditation and breakfast. It was, after all, my only chance to enjoy some winter recreation. Frequently, the chickadees would come by for food. Usually one of them would fly to a nearby branch and utter a "cheep" to inform me of his presence. Sometimes, simply to test the chickadee's response, I would ignore the first chirp and continue cleaning the steps. After a few moments, the chickadee would fly a little closer and utter another, louder "cheep". If I ignored this request, the chickadee would start buzzing me. Eventually I would give in, drop my snow shovel, dig a little jar of birdseed out of my jacket pocket, and offer the seeds to the hungry bird.

Considering how the chickadees would alter their behavior in response to my reactions, I must assume that they were behaving consciously. After all, they certainly were not behaving instinctively, as many materialists would contend, since wild birds do not have the instinct to feed out of a person's hand. One could argue that the chickadee's behavior was purely a response to rewards they were receiving, i.e. it was a type of behaviorism. Although their initial tendency to feed out of our hands may be a reward response, the way the birds changed their behavior to fit mine suggests that something more complex was involved.

There is growing experimental and observational evidence that other species of birds also have extensive intellectual abilities. For example, the African gray parrot can learn English and use it as a way to solve various cognitive tasks[16], and the New

Caledonian crow can design and use tools to solve problems[17]. These types of behaviors hint strongly that these birds are conscious of their actions.

If the chickadees, African Grey Parrot, and New Caledonian Crows are conscious, then from where did their consciousness come? It certainly could not have been an emergent property produced by the large number of synapses in their brains because parrots and crows have brains that are smaller than a lima bean and chickadees have a brain the size of a grain of rice. This observation that birds with a tiny brain could be conscious would belie the theories of the materialists, which state that consciousness is simply an emergent property produced by abundant synapses in human brains. These results are increasingly supporting Bergson's contention that all life is conscious; even an amoeba has consciousness. As he said:

> "...it would be as absurd to refuse consciousness to an animal because it has no brain as to declare it incapable of nourishing itself because it has no stomach[18]."

Because there is no clear evidence indicating that consciousness is restricted to humans and other advanced animals, spiritual practitioners maintain that consciousness transcends the body and that the complex neural networks of our brains do not produce our consciousness, but rather provide access to a consciousness that is already there.

IMPLICATIONS

The struggle to determine which view of reality is correct has been an intellectual problem that has troubled Western society for centuries. Materialists contend that the way that a rational approach to science has enhanced our quality of life clearly shows that their way of thinking is correct. However, because materialists and spiritual practitioners both postulate a material realm to reality, science, which studies only the material realm, cannot distinguish between the view of reality postulated by materialists and that postulated by spiritualists. Thus, it is impossible to determine which view is correct simply through the study of natural phenomena. True, materialists and spiritual people have different concepts of how life and consciousness arise, but those are both questions that are not answerable by science. As noted above, we have no objective way of measuring consciousness. Even while using sophisticated brain imaging processes to monitor consciousness, as will be discussed in chapter four, scientists studying the brain run up against the problem of *qualia*. Qualia is the experience a person has of being conscious, such as the taste of sugar. Cognitive sciences can monitor the electrical activity of a person's brain and might be able to see some portion of the brain light up when the person tastes sugar. In other words, they might be able to obtain an objective image of brain activity, but they cannot know the subjective experience that person is having, without, of course, asking the subject of the study what she is experiencing. Because it is difficult to determine if animals are conscious, we cannot know how far down the chain of existence it goes. It is quite unscientific to assume without any convincing evidence that it is restricted to higher animals.

The problem of determining the processes that make life alive is also intractable to science. Experiments have shown that complex organic chemicals necessary for life could have been formed by natural processes in the reducing atmosphere of early Earth[19]. However, to date, scientists have not yet been able to create life in the lab. Maybe, sometime in the future, someone will be able to create life and to show with thermodynamic rigor how life must form by the correct combination of organic chemicals in the correct environment. In the meantime, however, the nature of the "vital force" (or the emergent property that causes life to be alive) will be speculative at best. In other words, science, because it relates entirely to the physical world, is totally blind when dealing with the spiritual world. As a result, science cannot be used to argue that the spiritual dimension does not exist and that reality is exactly as the materialists postulate it to be.

It is critical to establish which view of reality is correct, because, if the materialists are correct, the only worthwhile intellectual endeavor for humans lies in the field of science (and its related fields of medicine and engineering). In education, these fields go by the modern acronym STEM: Science-Technology-Engineering-Math. This classification implies that people who study aspects of the mind—philosophy, psychology and religion—are at best wasting their time. Remember, as noted in the quotes above, to materialists, the mind is just the brain. At worst, those people are misleading the rest of humanity. Those working in the humanities—art, literature, and music—are similarly suspect, since those disciplines have no material benefit to science or to a technological society.

However, if the spiritual view of reality is correct, then there are two important routes of intellectual investigation humans can follow: investigation of the outer world through science and the investigation of the inner world through religion and the humanities. The importance of science to our society goes without saying; it is the driving force of our economy, it underlies our health system, and it provides ways for ordinary humans to communicate with each other that would have seemed magical even a generation ago. However, studies of humanities and religion are equally important. To spiritual people, the world has far more meaning than the flat reality presented by the STEM curriculum. It is the understanding of that meaning, which can only be accessed through metaphor, allegory, music or images, that gives significance to human life.

CHAPTER 2

The Religious Experience

The materialistic view that reality consists only of that which we can see or measure is by far simpler than the spiritual view that reality consists of both a physical and a spiritual dimension. If one applies Occam's Razor, or the law of parsimony, which states that, given competing hypotheses, the one with the fewest assumptions is most likely to be valid, then the materialistic view should be accepted. This is one of the major arguments of materialists. Occam's Razor, of course, is compelling only if all the assumptions in the arguments are valid. Spiritual people maintain that there is a spiritual dimension to life because they have had an experience indicating that the mind is transcendent to the body. This experience is known as the religious, spiritual, or mystical experience; spiritual people would maintain that one cannot develop a unified view of reality without taking this experience into account.

The religious experience is very common. Written records of spiritual experiences go back thousands of years and are present in all religions. A 2009 survey by the *Pew Forum on Religion & Public Life* indicates 49% of the American public have had a religious experience[20]. The experience is not uniformly distributed across the population. Nearly 70% of white evangelicals and black Protestants have had a religious experience, whereas only around 40% of Catholics and main-line Protestants have had one. Interestingly, 18% of people who described themselves as atheists, agnostics, and 'secular unaffiliated' report having had a spiritual experience.

VARIETIES OF RELIGIOUS EXPERIENCE

A huge variety of religious experiences have been documented by many religious texts. One end of the spectrum involves simply a sudden insight into something one has known for a long time that is not accompanied by any unusual visual or auditory aspects. Take, for example, this experience of Martin Luther:

> "When a fellow monk," said Luther, "one day repeated the words of the Creed: 'I believe in the forgiveness of sins.' I saw the scripture in an entirely new light, and straight away, I felt as if I was born anew. It was as if I found the door of paradise thrown wide open[21]."

Another type of experience is the simple feeling that one is in the presence of another consciousness, as in this description:

> I had a revelation last Friday evening. I was at Mary's and happened to say something about the presence of spirits (of whom, I said, I was often dimly aware). Mr. Putnam entered into an argument with me on spiritual matters. As I was speaking, the whole system rose up before me like a vague destiny looming from the Abyss. I never before so clearly felt the spirit of God in me and around me. The whole room seemed to me full of God. The air seemed to waver to and fro with the presence of Something I knew not what. I spoke with the calmness and clearness of a prophet. I cannot tell you what this revelation was. I have not yet studied it enough. But I shall perfect it one day and then you shall hear it and acknowledge its grandeur[22].

Another type of experience is purely visual:

> All at once, without warning of any kind, I found myself wrapped in a flame-colored cloud. For an instant I thought of fire, an immense conflagration somewhere close by in that great city; the next I knew that the fire was within myself. Directly afterward there came upon me a sense of exultation, of immense joyousness accompanied by or immediately followed by an intellectual

illumination impossible to describe. Among other
things I did not merely come to believe, but I saw
that the universe is not composed of dead matter,
but is on the contrary a living Presence...[23]

The experience attained in deep meditation described by Lama
Shang (1123-1193) might fit into this purely visual type of
experience: He starts out by describing how it feels to be in deep
meditation, then gives over to the experiences that arise:

> The mind rests, immovable and stable,
> like the depths of the ocean.
>
> Then there will come experiences:
> experiences, of clarity, nonthought and bliss,
> like the center of space.
>
> There is undistracted self-illumination,
> like a lamp's flame undisturbed by wind.
>
> There is lucidity, vividness, and ease,
> like a rainfall of beautiful flowers.
>
> There is brightness, evenness, insubstantiality,
> like the sun shining in cloudless sky.
>
> There is transparency and purity,
> like a bronze vessel filled with water.

Recognizing that one cannot really impart the nature of the religious experience simply by words to others who have not had it, Lama Shang ends his description with a disclaimer noting that his description is NOT the same as the experience itself:

> There is no end to words like these.
>
> They have no basis, appearing like dream.
>
> They are insubstantial, appearing like rainbows.
>
> They are ungraspable, appearing like the moon on water...[24]

Another type of religious experience is purely audial, such as the experience of Saint Francis of Assisi. While visiting the chapel of San Damiano outside of Assisi, a voice from a crucifix of Jesus Christ said to him three times:

> "Francis, Francis, go and repair My house which, as you can see, is falling into ruins[25]."

An experience that was both audial and visual is that experience of Saul of Tarsus. Saul, a Jew who persecuted members of the new Christian sect, was on his way to Damascus to bring Christian prisoners to Jerusalem for punishment. On his journey, he had the following experience:

> While I was on my way and approaching Damascus, about noon a great light from heaven suddenly shone about me.

I fell to the ground and heard a voice saying to me, 'Saul, Saul, why are you persecuting me?'

I answered, 'Who are you Lord?' Then he answered me, 'I am Jesus of Nazareth whom you are persecuting.'

Now those who are with me saw the light but did not hear the voice of the one who was speaking to me.

I asked, 'What am I to do Lord?' The Lord said to me, 'Get up and go to Damascus; there you will be told everything that has been assigned to you to do.'

Since I could not see because of the brightness of that light, those who were with me took my hand and led me to Damascus[26].

After arriving in Damascus, a Christian by the name of Ananias laid his hands upon Saul and cured his blindness. After this event, Saul adopted his Roman name, Paul, and spent more than 20 years preaching Christianity throughout the eastern Roman Empire.

Some experiences may even involve a trance-like state. A good example of this type of experience is a description by Ramakrishna, a Hindu mystic who lived in Bengal from 1836 until 1886:

> O Beloved companions, what uncharted regions of Divine Ecstasy I have passed through! I can only express a particle to you through words. When I begin to recount certain very secret experiences, Mother paralyzes my tongue and I simply cannot form words, although I am fervently longing to share these treasures with you.
>
> After I first received the direct vision of Mahakali, my blissful mother—Her scintillating Black Form rising out of a golden ocean, with gigantic waves rushing at me from all sides—I remained in a constant visionary state. It was literally impossible for me to tell any difference between night and day, so brilliant was Her Radiance, permeating my mind and senses. Undiscerning persons considered me insane. They dubbed me "the mad priest of Dakshineswar". But my madness was the sweet madness of Divine Love, free from the bitterness characteristic of mental and emotional derangement[27].

Some of the most complex religious experiences were those that affected Muhammad. One night in 610 A.D. he awoke to find himself overwhelmed by a devastating presence that squeezed him tightly until he heard the first verses of what later turned out to be the Quran emerging from his lips:

> It is no less than inspiration sent down to him:
>
> He was taught by one Mighty in Power,
>
> Endued with Wisdom: for he appeared
> (in stately form);
>
> While he was in the highest part of the horizon:
>
> Then he approached and came closer,
>
> And was at a distance of but two bow-lengths or
> (even) nearer[28].

The Quran was revealed to Muhammad over the next 21 years; most of the revelations were painful to Muhammad and were associated with convulsions[29].

THE RELIGIOUS EXPERIENCE AND MYSTICISM

Perhaps the best discussion of the nature of religious experiences is given in William James' book *The Varieties of Religious Experience,* which has lost none of its vitality in the century since it was written. James points out that the mystical experience has the following properties: it is ineffable; it is noetic; it is transient, it lasts for seconds to minutes; and it is passive, which means that it comes upon the person experiencing it spontaneously.

The experience is ineffable, or indescribable, not because it is too subtle to put into words, but because our language does not have the words to describe it. To understand this problem, consider what it would be like if you were blind and lived in a world where everyone else was also blind. The language that you would have learned would contain a lot of words for tactile experiences, but none for visual experiences. What would happen if, for a few moments, you were granted with the ability to see? You would see an amazing world that exists far outside your realm of touch. There would be colors and details everywhere; a blue sky, white clouds, and green trees. The experience would be vivid, but the trouble is, how would you describe it to others when your language has no word for colors, sky or clouds? Mystics encounter the same problem with the spiritual experience—our vocabulary has no words to describe the experience. The best one can do is to hint at it using symbols, similes, or metaphors.

The religious experience is noetic. This means that, even if one cannot describe it in words, intellectually one realizes that it carries a deep meaning. In the example above, although one cannot describe the experience where one suddenly gained vision, it would carry a great importance, even if it lasted for a few moments. It will tell one that there is a whole dimension of experience that exists outside of one's every-day awareness. Even after the experience passed, the realization that this visual dimension exists would stay with one, even if one never experienced it again. Indeed, it is likely that, for the rest of one's life, one will endeavor to understand both the experience and the visual dimension it revealed to one.

This is exactly what happens to people who undergo the mystical experience. They have been given the realization that much more exists in life than the "reality" presented by the phenomenal world but the short taste that they received from the experience is not enough to satiate the drive toward understanding the mystery the experience was trying to show. In her book *Mysticism,* Evelyn Underhill discusses four characterizations of the path that mystics follow to understand the dimension that the spiritual experience had opened to them:

1. True mysticism is active and practical, not passive and theoretical. It is an organic life process, a something that the whole self does; not something to which its intellect holds an opinion.

2. Its aims are wholly transcendental and spiritual. It is in no way concerned with adding to, exploring, re-arranging, or improving anything in the visible universe. The mystic brushes away that universe, even its supernormal manifestations. Though he does not, as his enemies declare, neglect his duty to the many, his heart is always set upon the changeless One.

3. This One is for the mystic, not only the Reality of all that is, but also a living and personal Object of Love: never an object of exploration. It draws his whole being homeward, but always under the guidance of the heart.

4. Living union with this One—which is the term of his adventure—is a definite state or form of enhanced life. It is obtained neither from intellectual realization of its delights, nor from the most acute emotional longings. It is arrived at by an arduous psychological and spiritual progress—the Mystic Way—entailing the complete remaking of character and the liberation of a new, or rather latent, form of consciousness; which imposes on the self the condition which is sometimes inaccurately called "ecstasy," but is better named the Unitive State[30].

The mystic path, therefore, is not merely an intellectual process, but rather a process that involves the complete change in one's personality so that the mystic can better experience the truths that the spiritual experience has hinted at so alluringly.

True, most religious people are not mystics, but because mysticism is the core of religion, the mystic path is a key endmember of the spectrum describing the human response to the divine. As such, it provides an important insight into the nature of religion that materialists cannot understand. To paraphrase Underhill, religion is an intense experience, not simply an intellectual affirmation of belief, a point that is a direct contradiction to the arguments that atheists make about religion.

RATIONAL THOUGHT AND RELIGION

As noted frequently in the preceding pages, the understanding of religion is based upon experience, and this means is that rational arguments can never *prove* the existence of the divine, just as one cannot prove the taste of sugar simply by rational discourse. James is quite adamant about this:

> What religion reports, you must remember, always purports to be a fact of experience: the divine is actually present, religion says, and between it and ourselves relations of give and take are actual. If definite perceptions of fact like this cannot stand on their own feet, surely abstract reasoning cannot give them the support they are in need of. Conceptual processes can class facts, define them, interpret them; but they do not produce them or reproduce their individuality...

> In all sad sincerity I think we must conclude that the attempt to demonstrate by purely intellectual processes the truth of deliverances of direct religious experience is absolutely hopeless[31].

James also points out that rational proof about the existence of the divine only makes sense to those who have already had a religious experience.

> The truth is that in the metaphysical and religious sphere, articulate reasons are cogent for us only when our inarticulate feelings of reality have already been impressed in favor of the same conclusions[32].

This nicely explains why, although religious scholars have tried for centuries to prove the existence of God, their reasonings continue to fall on deaf ears as far as materialists are concerned. Because materialists have not been primed by a religious experience, they cannot understand the subtexts of the arguments.

A good example of this problem is the argument from desire. This argument is summarized thus:

> **PREMISE 1:** Every innate desire points to an object of satisfaction.

> **PREMISE 2:** We have an innate desire that only God can satisfy.

> **CONCLUSION:** Therefore, God exists[33].

This argument makes perfect sense to me. I have been seeking to understand the experience that I had in the snowy New Jersey woods nearly sixty years ago. The argument, however, would make no sense at all to a materialist who is convinced that the religious experience is some sort of anomaly in the function of our brains. If a materialist had a mystical experience himself (or herself), he (or she) would probably have dismissed it as an effect of poorly digested meat, much as Scrooge dismissed the first appearance Marley's ghost in *A Christmas Carol.* By dismissing the significance of their own experience, materialists clearly see no reason to seek an explanation for it.

Obviously if one cannot prove by reasoning that the divine exists, one cannot prove by logic that it doesn't exist either. As is inherent in James' arguments, one's religious faith is built upon experience, and there is no way that anyone can prove that another person's experience is not meaningful. A good example of this is the herb cilantro, which adds spice to Mexican cooking. Although I like the taste of it, some people hate it. To them, it tastes like soap. I can use all the arguments I want to argue that cilantro is a valuable addition to Mexican dishes and that it enhances other flavors, but my arguments will not convince someone for whom cilantro tastes awful. Likewise, all the rational arguments that materialists use to disregard the religious experience look hollow to someone who has had such an experience.

LINEAR THINKING VS.
HOLISTIC THINKING

As noted above, the mystic path involves distinct psycholog-ical changes. One important change is how one thinks about the world. The Greek word for this change is *metanoia*, which is translated as "changing one's mind". This means literally changing the way one views reality. In the modern Western world, most people are linear thinkers. Linear thinking is very important when dealing with the world of mathematics, science, or engineering. Over the past few centuries, science has estab-lished many measurements and laws; the force of gravity is the same (at least at the first approximation) everywhere around the world. The atomic weight of the elements is well known as is the tensile strength of most metals. Linear thinking can be consid-ered "either-or" thinking; either a scientific hypothesis fits one's understanding of the available data or it does not. If careful calculations show that the design of a bridge cannot stand up to the stresses that it will be subjected to when it is finished, clearly it is foolish to build it.

Although linear thinking works well when dealing with objects, it is not efficient when dealing with people. That is because, instead of comparing information to a set of uniform rules, as would happen in a scientific study, there are no uniform rules to apply when considering human relations. The data most people use for comparison to or evaluation of others comes from their own ego: their experiences, feelings, and prejudices. Our egos are very sensitive, which is understandable, since they evolved as a way to keep us alive. When encountering a new situation, the first thought we are likely to have is, "Will this situation harm me, be beneficial to me, or is it neutral?" Unfortunately, we do this with people as well as with experiences; we immediately judge whether that person looks sympathetic to us or whether she is likely to be hostile. In this way, linear thinking, by definition, divides the world into two parts—"us", the good guys who agree with me, and "them", the bad guys who do not.

Although atheists and fundamentalists are intellectual enemies, they have one characteristic in common: they want certainty.

> Both seek knowledge with a sure foundation—
> that of logic and sense data, in the one case, that
> of infallible scripture in the other[34].

A good example of this need for certainty is this quote:

> ...I'm a skeptic not because I do not want to
> believe, but because I want to *know*. How can we
> tell the difference between what we would like to
> be true and what is actually true?

> The answer is science. We live in the Age of Science,
> in which beliefs are supposed to be grounded in
> rock-solid evidence and empirical data[35].

Certainty is, of course, what linear thinking is all about. As I said above, if one is building a bridge, one uses linear thinking to check the designs to be certain that it won't collapse. However, this is not the kind of thinking upon which religion has been built. One might be certain that one had a religious experience, but because the experience is ineffable, one cannot be certain about how to describe it. This is the reason why mystics commonly are humble people: they know that they have had experiences that cannot be described.

We are used to looking at reality in a dualistic manner. In this context, dualism means that there are two aspects to reality, the outside world and the person who is experiencing it. We all carry around a sense of "me", which is the subject that is experiencing the world. And we all assume that there is a world out there that we are experiencing, which is entirely separate from "me". Mystics of all traditions tell that this way of viewing reality is false. They tell of reaching a point where the sense of having a separate self falls away and there is no difference between themselves and their experience. In other words, during this experience, the ego, the window through which the mystic views the world, becomes transparent. This is called the non-dualistic experience, and it leads to holistic or paradoxical thinking[36]. The paradox comes from the fact that mystics may realize that the sense of "me" is a fabrication, but they also realize that the sense of "me" is necessary for them to operate in the world. When the ego is not present, or to be more precise, when one can see through the ego, one gets holistic thinking, which allows one to see all sides of an argument without adhering to any one of them.

Karen Armstrong has called linear and holistic thinking *logos* and *mythos*[37]. "Logos" is the Greek term for logical thinking, the linear thinking described above, whereas "mythos" is a term that describes thinking through symbols and metaphors, which is the holistic thinking. It doesn't matter what one calls these ways of thinking, the key thing is that there are two ways of viewing the world, one of which is the highly rational process that has become the main approach used in modern society, and the other is the metaphorical or holistic way that is key to understanding religion.

Here is how I got a sense of what holistic thinking is all about. For months on retreat we were encouraged to look out the window in our room as we meditated while trying to experience the vivid world outside as "appearance emptiness", a term that to me seemed quite opaque. One blustery day in February of my last year of retreat, I was sitting in my room trying to see bare appearance in the reality that was outside my windows. Snow squalls were blowing in from the Gulf of St. Laurence, sweeping up the cliff, and buffeting the walls of the retreat center. Whenever a gust of snow-laden wind blew by my window, the trees that lined the top of the cliff faded into white, only to appear again a few moments later as the gust blew by. As I watched the blowing snow drift by I tried to maintain a stable mind and simply see what was outside my window. Suddenly I saw the trees and the blowing snow as merely white and green shapes. In a flash I realized that I was seeing appearance emptiness and that the trees and snow were simply concepts that my mind had placed on simple visual phenomena.

The Buddhist view of perception is that input from our senses is transmitted to our brain by electrical pulses in our nerves and in the brain that they are reconstructed into the sense of sight, sound, taste, etc. In other words, any experience we are having with the "outside world" actually takes place in our mind. The visual experiences actually appear in our minds as appearance emptiness—appearances that are empty of any meaning. It is only when they are processed by our mind that they become loaded with concepts. I was seeing white and green shapes; it was my mind that interpreted those appearances as snow blowing in front of trees.

The evidence that perception actually works by seeing the world as "appearance emptiness" is demonstrated by the fact that people who have had their sight restored after being blind from birth have problems interpreting their visual experience. For many of them, what they see makes no sense. These people see shapes and colors, but they have no way of interpreting them. Babies spend much of their time in the first months of their lives learning how to interpret the information that their senses are conveying to them. They learn the nature and limits to objects, they learn perspective, and how to maneuver in a three-dimensional world. A blind person who gets vision restored later in life has bypassed that learning experience and has to learn how to see. Some of them never manage to do it and behave as if they are blind even years after they have had vision restored[38].

A blind person who has gained vision in her twenties sees what I saw that snowy day on retreat—appearance emptiness. The appearance describes the shapes that she was seeing, while the emptiness was the fact that she had not learned how to interpret the experience. The only difference between her experience and mine is that I had to undo a lifelong habit before I could see

that way. No wonder that spiritual training is so extremely difficult—we are trying to undo deeply ingrained habits!

As soon as I realized that what I saw was overlain by concepts,
I became aware that EVERYTHING I experience is also overlain by concepts, not only my visual experience of the trees and
blowing snow. The sounds I hear are simply pressure waves in
the air. It is my mind that interprets them as fine music, the
caw of a crow, or the moaning of the wind. All of my feelings about who I like and who I don't, my politics, my views of
science and religion are concepts that are colored by my ego. As
soon as I became aware of this, the solidity of all my opinions
melted and I began to see the world with holistic, rather than
linear, thinking.

Holistic thinking is "both-and" thinking. Unlike linear thinking,
which is inherently judgmental, holistic thinking, being freed
from seeing through the ego-filter, is distinctly non-judgmental.
As noted above, the first thing one's ego does when faced with a
new person is to judge whether the person is likely to be a threat.
Thus, holistic thinking, thinking without the ego, is clearly the
kind of thinking Jesus was describing when he said, "Do not
judge, so that you may not be judged."[39]

The development of holistic or paradoxical thinking is a critical
need before a person can be non-judgmental and can develop
the kind of personality that is advocated by the world's wisdom
traditions.

As the Franciscan friar Richard Rohr says:

> Non-polarity thinking (if you prefer that phrase) teaches you how to hold creative tensions, how to live with paradox and contradictions, how not to run from mystery, and therefore how to actually practice what all religions teach as necessary: compassion, mercy, loving kindness, patience and humility[40].

Holistic thinking is the root of religion because it is much easier to deal with difficult people or situations in a skillful manner when one's ego is not in the way. It is also the root of humility, because with holistic thinking, one is no longer projecting one's ego into situations and one can afford to step back and deal with those situations in a skillful manner.

CHAPTER 3

The Nature of Religion

INTRODUCTION

The dispute about the nature of reality described in chapter one is being played out within two institutions in society—religion, which is the study of the spiritual realm, and science, the study of the material world. In the next two chapters, I will discuss what religion and science each can and cannot tell us about the nature of reality. In this chapter I will discuss the strengths and weaknesses of religion. In the next, I will cover science and what it tells us about reality.

Perhaps the best definition of religion comes from the Snowmass Conference, a conference that was held in 1984 at St. Benedict's

Monastery in Snowmass, Colorado, and which continued yearly at various other venues until 2004. The conferences involved spiritual teachers from the Buddhist, Hindu, Islamic, Jewish, Native American, Russian Orthodox, Protestant, and Roman Catholic faiths.[41] One of the results of these conferences is a list of eight features that are common to all religions:

1. The World's Religions bear witness to the experience of Ultimate Reality to which they give various names: Brahman, Allah, (the) Absolute, God and the Great Spirit. The key word in this sentence is "experience". The world's religions are not elaborate fairy tales about how the world came to be, as most atheists would maintain. Rather, religions are based upon an experience that conveys a sense of unity with nature, an infusion of love for the beings within it, and a feeling of certainty that there is a deep meaning to life.

2. Ultimate Reality cannot be limited by any name or concept. Because Ultimate Reality lies beyond words, we cannot describe it with words; we can only hint at it with symbols. This is why holistic thinking is necessary to understand the metaphysical language and symbolism of the holy texts. Similarly, the rituals and ceremonies of religions must be seen as symbols of the Ultimate Reality. The fact that Islam uses 99 attributes for Allah is a recognition that an accurate description of Ultimate Reality cannot be conveyed easily with words.

3. Ultimate Reality is the ground of infinite potentiality and actualization. This means that much of our creativity and insight, and indeed our consciousness itself, comes from

Ultimate Reality. This is a recognition that, in addition to having an outer, or transcendent manifestation, Ultimate Reality also has an inner, or immanent manifestation. A good description of this has been given by Wayne Teasdale:

> The mystery of the outer and inner is that they have the same ground of identity: they are the same...The same divine reality that holds the universe within itself also dwells in our hearts, in the deepest part of our subjectivity, in the very act of our arising to awareness within us. The divine presence immanent in the whole universe, in the natural world, in life and being also inhabits the depths of our inner life[42].

The existence of an immanent as well a transcendent aspect to Ultimate Reality explains why inner religious practices, such as prayer or meditation, can result in the understanding of the transcendent nature of Ultimate Reality.

4. Faith is opening, accepting, and responding to Ultimate Reality. Faith in this sense precedes every belief system. Although modern discussion of religion usually considers the words "faith" and "belief" to be synonyms, there is an important difference between the two. In many ways, "belief" can be considered the opposite of "faith". As the Buddhist teacher Sharon Salzberg points out:

> Faith, in contrast to belief, is not a definition of
> reality, not a received answer, but an active, open
> state that makes us willing to explore[43].

Similarly, Anthony DeMello, the Jesuit mystic, says, "Beliefs give you a lot of security, but faith is insecurity[44]." *Faith* produces insecurity because it opens one to something that is unknown and indescribable. It involves being open to the inexpressible experiences that arise when one begins to get in touch with Ultimate Reality. In contrast, *belief* involves ossifying these inexpressible experiences into solid symbols.

5. The potential for human wholeness—or enlightenment, salvation, transcendence, transformation, blessedness—is present in every human being. Enlightenment or salvation is a human birthright that is accessible to everyone; it is not a product that is restricted to any particular religion, race, or civilization. Even though it is a birthright, for most of us this wholeness is hidden; it requires years of spiritual practice before one can claim this inheritance.

6. Ultimate Reality may be experienced not only through religious practices but also through nature, art, human relationships, and service to others. Although religious practices are usually lauded as providing access to the experience of Ultimate Reality, they are not the only path toward that experience. There are numerous reports in literature about people transcending their egos through experiences that lie outside of formal religion. A vivid example of this would be the experience I had in the snowy New Jersey woods many years ago. It certainly had nothing to do with religious practice, because I was an atheist at the time.

7. As long as the human condition is experienced as separate from Ultimate Reality, it is subject to ignorance and illusion, weakness and suffering. Without a spiritual view of life, human beings are immersed in their own ego, which presents a highly biased view of how the world should be. The ego wants to be happy, and it has a list of things it needs to bring about that happiness. Unfortunately, life doesn't always produce the things that the ego is yearning for, which means that life lived in this manner is often deeply disappointing. Once one has experienced the Ultimate Reality, the wants and wishes of the ego look very petty, and one can absorb the disappointments of life with equanimity. Even death, which is the ultimate insult to the ego, can be accepted because one has a visceral understanding that the mind is a manifestation of the spiritual dimension, which is not extinguished at death.

8. Disciplined practice is essential to the spiritual life, yet spiritual attainment is not the result of one's own efforts, but the result of the experience of oneness with Ultimate Reality. At first reading, this point sounds a little depressing. Although spiritual practices are important for spiritual attainment, the attainment is not solely the product of one's efforts. Instead, one's spiritual practice makes one open to mystical insights. In Christian terms, attainment arises through the process of grace, or as a Buddhist friend said, "Enlightenment arises by error; meditation makes you error-prone."

THE ENTRAPMENT OF CONCEPTS

Ultimate Reality lies beyond concept, but religions must rely on concepts to describe it. This is a necessary compromise, because without concepts one cannot develop a set of doctrines, symbols, or rituals that are meant to lead practitioners toward direct experience of the ineffable. Unfortunately, it is a devil's compromise because it is very easy for one to fall into the misconception that the doctrines and symbols, which are meant to direct one toward the experience of Ultimate Reality, are actually the Ultimate Reality itself. This problem is a curse that has tormented religion throughout its history. As a traditional Zen saying puts it dramatically:

> "When the wise man points at the moon
> All the fool sees is the finger."

Because of this tendency for people to mistake the finger for the moon, religion, which should bring peace, has engendered differences, which sometimes have led to hatred, oppression, and warfare. It is as if many fingers were pointing at the moon but each religion saw only its own finger. Sadly, those people who are fighting over which religion is the best are totally unaware that they are fighting over the nature of the finger; they may not even be aware that the moon exists.

The Varieties of Religions

Because Ultimate Reality lies beyond all concepts, each religion has developed its own doctrines, symbols, and rituals to describe it. This explains the amazing variety of religions in the world. How each person experiences Ultimate Reality depends strongly on his or her cultural background. A Muslim praying to Allah is unlikely to have visions of the Shiva, nor is a Catholic likely to have visions of Muhammad. The protean nature of the religious experience is well demonstrated by the life of Ramakrishna. Ramakrishna was a devotee of the Hindu goddess Kali and, as described in chapter two, was commonly enveloped in rapture while praying to her. During one period in his life Ramakrishna took up Islamic practice. He removed all Hindu images from his room, chanted verses of the Quran in Arabic, and performed the cycles of prostrations praising Allah as Muslims do every day. After a short time he was graced with a vision of Muhammad who merged with his being and lifted his awareness to a mystic union with Allah. Another time while gazing on a painting of the Virgin Mary, a sense of Christ's nature came forth from the icon and penetrated into the heart of his consciousness. He was so taken by this that he couldn't enter the temple to Kali for three days[45].

Although it is rare to find humans who are as spiritually adept as Ramakrishna, the stories about him dramatically show that the practices and stories of each religion are meant to direct practitioners toward the religious experience. This means that the sacred stories of each religion are pointing to an experience that one cannot understand until one has experienced it oneself.

Consequently, no religion has the sole answer to the nature of Ultimate Reality. Because it is inherently impossible to describe the experience completely, each religion has developed its own ways to hint at the nature of that experience, but this doesn't invalidate the approach of other religions.

A good example of the variety of religious expression is the way the world's religions envision the nature of Ultimate Reality. When most members of Western society think of religion, they think of a personal God. It is difficult for most Westerners to understand that a number of religions, Buddhism and Taoism foremost among them, are non-theistic. In non-theistic religions Ultimate Reality has no personality. The theistic religions, Judaism, Christianity, and Islam, which worship a transcendent loving creator, appear to be an entirely different species than the non-theistic religions. It seems impossible for theistic and non-theistic religions to have any common root. However, these contrasting views of Ultimate Reality coexist quite easily in Hinduism, one of the world's oldest religions. Depending on one's proclivities, a good Hindu may worship Nirguna Brahman (God without attributes) or Saguna Brahman (God with attributes). Huston Smith uses the following analogy to compare theistic and non-theistic approaches to the Ultimate Reality:

> If one is struggling against a current, it is comforting to have a master swimmer by one's side. It is equally important that there be a shore, solid and serene, that lies beyond the struggle as the terminus of one's splashings[46].

Ken Wilber in his book, *Integral Spirituality*, maintains that this paradox arises because Ultimate Reality manifests as first, second and third person. The first-person manifestation is the feeling one has when having a religious experience. The second-person manifestation is the sense of a loving God that is inherent in the theistic religion. The third-person manifestation is the sense of Godhead, the Ultimate from which all reality arises, which is the sense of deity described by the non-theistic religions.

The Perennial Philosophy

The recognition that each religion is merely a finger pointing at the moon is a statement of the *perennial philosophy*, a term that was first defined by the German philosopher Gottfried Wilhelm Leibniz (1646–1716). The expression was made popular by Aldous Huxley in his 1945 book entitled *Perennial Philosophy*. It has also been referred to as *perennial wisdom* and *perennialism*. The eight points defining religion from the Snowmass conference quoted at the beginning of this chapter comprise a statement of perennialism. These points can be simplified to three concepts:

1. The world is pervaded by a spiritual reality that carries different names in different religions.

2. The world's religions provide paths toward experiencing that reality, and

3. The major goal of a person's life is to experience that spiritual truth.

One important point to emphasize is that perennialism does *not* indicate that all religions are the same, as some critics would maintain[47]. This conclusion should be obvious from the fact, as discussed above, that the world's religions involve both theistic and non-theistic traditions. Clearly the doctrines of theistic and non-theistic religions are very different, yet both types of religion can still be considered fingers pointing at the moon.

BELIEF, FAITH, AND THE TWO MODES OF THINKING

As noted at the beginning of the chapter, there is a subtle but significant difference between the meanings of the words "faith" and "belief". Recognizing that humans have two ways of thinking about reality, linear thinking and holistic thinking, makes the differences between these two words more understandable. Karen Armstrong, argues that the word "belief", as we know it, wasn't even in the original Bible (in the quote below, the parentheses are those of the author, the square brackets are mine).

> When the Bible was translated into English, *credo* [I give my heart] and *pisteuo* [faith] became "I believe" in the King James version (1611). But the word "belief" has since changed its meaning. In Middle English *bileven* meant "to praise, to value, to hold dear." It was related to the German *belieben* ("to love"), *liebe* ("beloved"), and the Latin *libido*. So "belief" originally meant "loyalty to a person to whom one is bound in promise or duty."...

> During the late seventeenth century, however, as our concept of knowledge became more theoretical, the word "belief" started to be used to describe an intellectual assent to a hypothetical— and often dubious—proposition[48].

This change from "bileven" to "belief" during the seventeenth century clearly reflects the impact that the movement toward linear thinking has had on religion. As science became more significant in society in the seventeenth century, it became more important to "believe" the facts, postulations, and theories that science put forth. The accompanying feeling by many that one needed to believe in the literal truth of the sacred texts was one of the major impacts that materialism has had on religion.

As noted by Karen Armstrong, the acceptance of linear, rational thinking by Western society as a whole has led to the formation of fundamentalism, where the extent of one's religious faith became measured by the intensity of one belief in the literal truth of the scriptures[49]. Although the solidified nature of fundamentalism is far from the mystical aspects of many religions, this doesn't mean that one cannot obtain spiritual realization through practices derived from literal interpretations of holy texts; it is obvious that many have. Witness how nearly 70% of white evangelicals are reported to have had a religious experience, compared to 49% of the American population as a whole[50].

The problem with fundamentalism lies not in the literal interpretation of the Scripture, *per se*, but in how a person practicing fundamentalism relates to other religions. When one regards religion primarily through linear thinking, one is in danger of falling into an "us" versus "them" attitude, which is deleterious to spiritual development. As Richard Rohr says:

> This is exactly what Jesus is saying in chapter nine of John's Gospel. "Because you say, 'we see', you are blind."

> Religion has lost sight of Jesus' message here. It has not tended to create seekers or searchers, has not tended to create humble people who trust that God is always beyond them. We aren't focused on the great mystery. Rather religion has tended to create people who think that they have God in their pockets, people with quick, easy, glib answers. That's why so much of the West is understandably abandoning religion[51].

The most dangerous feature of linear thinking is that it allows one to fall into the sense that there are "true" religions (generally one that you are following) and "false" religions (those that others may follow). This sense of "true" versus "false" religions is divisive, as Rabbi Shapiro says:

> Religions aren't "true" or "false" but rather "healthy" or "unhealthy". Healthy religions are about universal wisdom and love, about providing meaning in a way that opens your heart, sharpens your mind, and unclenches your fists. Healthy

religions invite you to meet those of other religions and ask, "What can I learn from you?"
rather than "How can I get you to think like me?"

Unhealthy religions are about power and control,
imposing meaning in a manner that inhibits ques-
tioning, doubt, or learning from those labelled as
"other". Unhealthy religions worship conformity:
are you towing the line, staying true to tradition, upholding ancient opinions in the name of
sacred truths[52]?

Unfortunately, even if "unhealthy" religion is a minor aspect of
multifarious face of religion in western society, it certainly gets
a lot of press, and it is this publicity that partially accounts for
the decrease of interest in religion in the West.

THE PRE/TRANS FALLACY

Another way to understand the problem of how the modern
world relates to religion is to recognize that historically human
intellectual development has gone through three stages, which
range from the *pre-rational*, to the *rational* to the *trans-rational*[53].
In the pre-rational stage, one's view of reality is based upon
magic, myth and superstition. In the rational stage, one's view
of reality is based upon rational thinking. In the trans-rational
stage one accepts the rational reality of science, but considers it
relative reality. Trans-rational people also are aware of a spiritual
dimension to life, which is encompassed by Ultimate Reality. A
person who has a trans-rational view of reality has no problem

using rational thinking when dealing with relative reality, but when dealing with Ultimate Reality, that person's thinking lies beyond rational thought, hence the term trans-rational.

This three-fold classification for the stages of consciousness has an important impact on understanding the discussion of religion in the modern world. The materialist world view is firmly established within the rational stage of consciousness. There are many rational people who have had mystical experiences. They recognize that the experience involves mental processes that lie beyond those of the rational mind. Although these people may recognize the importance of rational thought in other aspects of life, they consider that the religious experience lies beyond rationality. Hence, they are considered to reside in the trans-rational stage.

Those who interpret religious doctrines literally and believe that, for example, the Earth is actually only 6,000 years old, consider reality through a mythic lens and lie within the pre-rational stage of consciousness. The reason for this is that, although reading the scriptures literally may mirror the rational approach of science, in the process of doing so, the person is forced into denying the veracity of the scientific view of reality. Consequently, the person is pushed into a pre-rational stage of consciousness.

Both pre-rational and trans-rational people are talking about spiritual experiences, but the distinction between pre-rational and trans-rational thinking is lost among many rational thinkers, who collapse the three stages of thought from pre-rational,

rational, and trans-rational to rational and irrational. Ken Wilber calls this the *pre/trans fallacy*[54].

> If you do not believe in Spirit, then you will take every trans-rational event and reduce it to pre-rational impulses and preverbal twaddle, perhaps claiming it is regressive, nothing but a holdover from the... days of infancy[55].

With this view, atheists will conclude:

> ...God is something you can simply outgrow, if you just keep trying. With this sleight of hand, this intellectual bit of laziness, all trans-rational realities are dismissed[56].

Much of the fire and fury relating to the conflict between atheists and religious people goes back to this pre/trans fallacy. By confusing pre-rational arguments with trans-rational ones, much of the depth, complexity, and wisdom of spiritual practices are hidden to atheists.

The pre/trans fallacy therefore is:

> ...a cultural catastrophe of the first magnitude. And yet, until religion itself learns how to convey these differences convincingly and learns to focus on the best in its... contemplative dimensions, religion for the world at large will likely remain

the province of either prerational fanatics or rational cynics[57].

In this discussion, the fundamentalist thinking is categorized as pre-rational, but this classification does not lessen the importance of the religious experiences of fundamentalists. The problem comes when they try to explain their inherently inexplicable experience to others, they couch their arguments in terms of literal interpretations of the Scriptures. As a result, they are forced into pre-rational arguments and those arguments do nothing to convince people who are firmly entrenched in the rational way of thinking that religion is a valid pursuit.

"I AM SPIRITUAL, BUT NOT RELIGIOUS"

The strident arch-conservatism of fundamentalism and the continual attacks by atheists implying that religion is an anti-intellectual endeavor have combined to decrease the influence of religion in Western society. In fact, religion has become so distasteful to many millennials that they say: "I am spiritual, but not religious." In some ways this statement "I am spiritual, but not religious" is positive because it indicates that even in this age of materialism, there are still many people who recognize the spiritual dimension to life, even if they do not consider that religions provide any access to it. However, the quote is also a negative statement, because the spiritual path requires intense discipline and extensive practice. Although the mystical portions of the world's religions are hidden to many people who do not participate in religion, they do provide access to the spiritual path. Religions provide practices that open one to the spiritual dimension and help one to develop the humility that comes with spiritual attainment. Unfortunately, the spiritual path is exceedingly difficult to find on one's own, and when one abandons institutions that might help one follow that path, one is in danger of becoming lost. This is a significant reason why the eclipsing of religion by modern materialism has been such a tragedy. Clearly, the major goal for religions in this century is to shake off the shackles of materialism and to show people that traditional religions still provide a pathway to spiritual realization.

CHAPTER 4

The Efficacy of Science

The scientific advances that have been made over the last few generations have produced a world that would be truly amazing to people living even two centuries ago. At the end of the seventeenth century people were living in much the way that humans had lived for millennia. True, the printing press had made books more available than they had been in the Middle Ages and information moved relatively swiftly through the advent of newspapers. Warfare was deadlier because of the invention of guns and cannons, but on the whole, people still lived as they had for centuries. The economy was largely based on agriculture and transportation was by foot, horse, or sailing ships. Medicine was rudimentary, meaning that life spans were relatively short.

Today we have a complex economy that has brought wealth to a large proportion of our society, we can communicate instantly to places half a world away, we can travel long distances in a few hours, and we have developed amazing medical techniques that allow us to cure many diseases that were previously considered incurable. There is little doubt that science is the driving force that keeps our economy running. Everything from the extraction and exploitation of energy and raw materials, to the development of new modes of transportation and of communication, and to the medical technology that promises us longer lives, requires a continued input from new scientific discoveries. It is little wonder, therefore, that many people have come to consider that the "either-or" way of thinking that is characteristic of science is the only reasonable way to examine the world.

THE "CONFLICT" BETWEEN SCIENCE AND RELIGION

It has become almost axiomatic in our culture to argue that science and religion are at war and that science is carrying the flag of modernity and tolerance against the forces of religion, which champion ignorance and intolerance. Many authors, however, maintain that this view, popular though it may be, is unreasonable and that the conflict between science and religion is actually a conflict between those who have extreme views of either religion or science[58]. The best example of this extreme view is that of the Young Earth Creationists who have created "creation science" because "normal" science doesn't agree with their literal interpretation of the Bible. The approach of

Christian fundamentalists to science has been called "paranoid science" and has been described this way:

> ...the paranoid science of the Christian Right actually claims to outdo mainstream science (that is real science) in factual analysis. Christian Right authors don't concede scientific truth, they create alternative science—that is an alternate reality—where their religious beliefs are safe from threat. In this alternative reality scientific data indicate that humans were intelligently designed by a creator, gays can be cured of their "illness", embryonic stem cell research is unnecessary for medical progress, and humans can consume all the fossil fuel they want to with no harmful effects on the environment. The anthropocentric universe based upon literal reading of the Bible is not only still plausible but supported by scientific investigation. Those who disagree are obviously driven by some sinister political motive, but certainly not by the pursuit of scientific truth[59].

This penchant of the fundamentalists to attack scientific theories that do not agree with a literal reading of the Bible has two effects. First, it fuels the idea that there is a conflict between science and religion, and second, it provides the atheists with a broad target, which they dutifully attack. The atheists assume that the literal interpretation of the Bible, which is the root of Young Earth Creationism, is typical of all religions. By basing religion entirely on belief in the literal truth of the Bible, rather than an experience of the Divine, the Young Earth Creationists make religion look like superstition (at least to the atheists). The Oxford dictionary defines *superstition* as:

> A widely held but irrational belief in supernatural influences, especially as leading to good or bad luck, or a practice based on such a belief.

It is clear that, because mystical religion is based upon the spiritual experience, it is not irrational. Certainly, the writings of theologians such as Thomas Aquinas are highly rational, but because the rationality of their arguments is built upon religious experiences as well as on objective facts, the arguments seem to be irrational to atheists. Unfortunately, when fundamentalists turn religion into belief in a literal interpretation of the Bible, they turn religion into something that looks very much like superstition.

PHILOSOPHICAL BASIS OF SCIENCE

One solid argument that the conflict between science and religion is more apparent than real comes from the fact that the philosophical basis of science is derived from the Judeo-Christian view of reality. This is summarized as:

I. **The world is good and worthy of study –**
    obviously one has to consider that the goals
    of science are worthy of pursuing before one
    begins to study it.

2. **The world is orderly and rational** – if the world was not orderly, then we would not be able to make any sense of it.

3. **The order of the world is open to the human mind** – One would not seek to understand the world it one didn't think it could be done.

4. **The order of the world is contingent rather than necessary** – necessary order is order that can be understood merely by rational thought, contingent order is order that must be ascertained by empirical methods.

5. **There is a real world out there to be studied** – This is a formulation of metaphysical realism, which is the concept that our senses are giving us information about a world that actually exists "out there".

6. **There is uniformity and unity to the physical universe** – this is the assumption that the laws of nature are uniform over time and space[60].

Each of the above statements is supported by Christian and Jewish beliefs; without this foundation, science would not have been able to develop[61]. The world-view established by Christianity in the Middle Ages was necessary for the birth of science, and hence, it is difficult to argue that there is a conflict between science and religion.

WHAT SCIENCE IS AND WHAT IT SAYS ABOUT REALITY

As noted in the previous chapter, materialists maintain that only through scientific knowledge can one obtain the certainty they crave about understanding the nature of reality. They contend that only the physical world is real and that this can be understood by pure reason, which is the root of science. To address the veracity of these arguments, I must first define what science is and show what science can and cannot say about the world around us.

SCIENCE AS A TECHNIQUE FOR SOLVING PROBLEMS. To make a simple definition, science provides us with a technique for solving problems, which is called the *scientific method*. Many people confuse "science" with the information that this problem-solving process has gleaned over the centuries. To understand the proper way to interpret the information that abounds in the lore of science, one must understand the technique of the scientific method. The scientific method involves three steps.

1. Observation of a physical phenomenon.

2. Postulation of a theory to explain the relations one has observed about this phenomenon.

3. Development of an experiment to test this theory.

There are four important constraints that accompany the scientific method.

1. Science obviously can only study those things that can be observed or measured. This means that science can only study the physical realm, it cannot observe, measure, or study the spiritual realm.

2. A theory is not scientific unless it can be tested. Karl Popper, the famous philosopher of science, called this property "falsifiability[62]." This means that for a theory to be scientific, one has to be able to prove it to be untrue. If a theory cannot be falsified, then it is not a scientific theory.

3. To be valid, an experiment must be reproducible. This means that other scientists must be able make similar experiments to test your results.

4. Although a set of experiments may disprove a theory, they can never *prove* one. In other words, there is always some sense of doubt about the theories of science and, as a result, scientific theories undergo continual modification as new concepts arise and new instruments are developed to study the phenomenal world.

The statements above have important implications to the arguments of both the fundamentalists and atheists. The statements show why "paranoid science" of the fundamentalists is not "science", because the purveyors of paranoid science pick and choose scientific facts and observations to *prove* their literal interpretation of the Bible. Their "scientific" theories cannot be falsified because, by definition, their types of science are not designed to be falsified; they are meant to prove the truth of the Bible. The statements above also belie the statement from materialists that was quoted previously, "in the Age of Science, beliefs must be grounded in rock-solid evidence and empirical data". The conclusions of science are NEVER proven. They are simply determined to be the best theory we have at the moment.

There are many aspects to science that do not fit into the belief materialists have that science is a rational process that provides one with a solid, factual view of the world. Most important are:

1. Certain aspects of science are indeterminate.

2. Scientific advances are commonly the results of non-rational processes. This includes the role of creativity in scientific insights and the role of scientific paradigms in determining the kinds of experiments that scientists do.

3. Science does not necessitate a materialistic view of the world.

ROLE OF DETERMINISM IN SCIENCE. The solid certainty of science advocated by the materialists harkens back to the kind of science that was around in the nineteenth century. Previous to the discovery of quantum physics, science was governed by Newtonian mechanics which implied that, given enough information about the state of the world, any future state could be predicted simply from the laws of physics. Unfortunately for this view of reality, in the early years of the twentieth century, physicists came to the distressing realization that, at the atomic scale, the physics of matter was determined by probability, chance, and uncertainty.

For example, radioactive elements such as uranium, known as parent elements, decay to daughter elements, such as lead, at a fixed rate called a half-life[63]. After one half-life, half of the atoms of the parent element would have decayed to the daughter element. If you had a powerful microscope that allowed you to look at a group of, perhaps ten, radioactive atoms there would be no way that you could tell which of those atoms would be the first to decay – it is totally a case of probability. Of course, at the scale of the world that we deal with, that probability is not important, we know that half of the parent atoms would have decayed after one half-life; when you are dealing with billions of atoms, it is not important which of those atoms would have decayed first.

The disappearance of determinism in the quantum world might have little impact on how materialists look at reality since, after all, quantum physics deals with a reality that lies well outside of the understanding and experience of most people. However, determinism, until fairly recently had also been an underpinning theory of biology. One of the major books advocating the deterministic, materialist view of life is put forth in Richard Dawkins' book *The Selfish Gene:*

> Like successful Chicago gangsters, our genes have survived, in some cases for millions of years, in a highly competitive world. This entitles us to expect certain qualities in our genes. I shall argue that a predominant quality to be expected in a successful gene is a ruthless selfishness. This gene selfishness will usually give rise to selfishness in individual behavior…Much as we would like to believe otherwise, universal love and welfare of the species as a whole are concepts that do not make evolutionary sense[64].

In his book, Dawkins advocated that genes control everything in life. The book carried the implication that the most important goal in life should be to pass one's genes on to the next generation. In such a model, people who have not had children, or those people whose children have grown up, provide very little value to society. The selfish gene theory was the ruling paradigm in biology for more than twenty years, but in recent years, the science of *epigenetics* has arisen. Epigenetics is a field of biology that shows how environmental signals acting on an organism can control the genes by turning some "on" and others "off". In the view of epigenetics:

Genes are simply molecular blueprints. And blueprints are simply design drawings; they are not the contractors that actually construct the building. Epigenetics functionally represents the mechanism by which the contractor selects appropriate gene blueprints and controls the construction and maintenance of the body[65].

Epigenetics shows that the role of genes in living beings is far more complex than the simplistic, deterministic selfish gene model. This means that the deterministic view of the "selfish gene" is a woefully unsophisticated view of how biological systems operate.

Another problem that arose in the quantum world is the fact that some features, most famously light and electrons, behave *both* as waves and particles. If you were to set up an experiment to determine if light or electrons were refracted, you would find that they behaved as waves. If you set up an experiment to measure the energy contained by light or electrons, you would conclude that they were particles. This means that our understanding of the quantum world comes from the kinds of experiments we design. In other words, our subjective experience plays a critical role in understanding the objective facts we observe about the quantum world.

The world of quantum physics leads to a huge problem for materialists. Not only does it mean that our subjective experience is important to understanding the physical world, it also implies that material objects don't really exist. Electrons do appear as solid objects, we can ascribe a charge to them and can count them as they move along a wire; after all, that is what the electrical unit of an ampere is. However, since electrons also exist as waves, it is obvious that they only appear as objects if we look at them that way. It may be very distressing to materialists, that, if one looks closely enough at any material object, one will find out that all it is made up of is energy. After all, that is what Einstein's famous equation $E = mc^2$ is telling us: Energy equals mass times the speed of light squared.

Finally, there is an unreducible uncertainty to the quantum world, which has been formulated as the famous Heisenberg Uncertainty Principle. According to the Heisenberg Uncertainty Principle, you can know either the location or the velocity of an electron, but not both. Any experiment you do to determine the location of an electron will disturb is velocity and vice versa.

When the materialists praise the certainty of science, they either have ignored the indeterminate nature of the quantum world, or they assumed that, the laws of quantum uncertainties simply do not apply in the physical world that we encounter with our senses. Even if we disregard the crazy things that go on in the quantum world, the reliable world of science that materialists describe does not exist. The suggestion that science takes objective observations and, by application of reason and logic, produces an answer about which one can be certain, simply does not describe how science really works.

Because science is dealing with objective data, materialists conclude that it is strictly an objective process. This is clearly not true because, if science were free from subjectivity, then all scientists looking at the same set of data would come to the same conclusion. Unfortunately, this is not so. Any scientist will tell you that the world of science is full of controversies that are as divisive and fiercely fought as any dispute in politics. The scientists involved in the controversies are all basing their theories on the same data. The difference comes from their subjective interpretation of those data.

SCIENCE AND CREATIVITY. Usually when one hears the word "creativity," one thinks of the subjective world of art or literature, rather than the rationality of science. However, creativity is equally as critical to science as it is to the humanities. The best scientist is not the person who can gather the most data, rather it is the person who can make the conceptual leap that explains trends that others had not previously recognized. In other words, although science is usually conceived of as involving an entirely logical process, it also involves a large component of intuition and creativity.

For example, although the scientific method looks like a simple logical process, in reality the method is considerably more complex. For many scientists the process of formulating a hypothesis about how a suite of data are related is a struggle that involves fumbling in the dark and chasing many dead ends. The answer commonly arises as a spontaneous insight. Once one has found the theory, one works backward to show how logic makes the theory fit the data[66].

One of the best examples of the use of intuition in science is Fredrich Kekulé's discovery of the structure of benzene in 1865. At the time that Kekulé was working on benzene, the science of chemistry knew very little about the structure of chemical compounds. Chemists could determine the composition of many compounds but how the atoms were put together to make those compounds was still a mystery. One of the group of compounds that scientists recognized at this time was the group of organic compounds known as alkanes. The simplest alkane is methane (CH_4), which is one carbon atom joined to four hydrogens. Next in complexity comes ethane (C_2H_6), in which two carbon atoms are joined together and surrounded by six hydrogen atoms. Then next in complexity is propane (C_3H_8), which consists of a chain of three carbon atoms bonded to eight hydrogen atoms. What is clear about these compounds is that they contain far more hydrogen than carbon; the compound with six carbon atoms, hexane (C_6H_{14}), contains 14 hydrogens. Benzene (C_6H_6), however, contains the same number of carbon atoms as does hexane but contains only six hydrogen atoms. How could this be? This is the problem that Kekulé was dealing with when:

> I was sitting, writing at my text books; but the work did not progress; my thoughts were elsewhere. I turned my chair to the fire and dozed. Again the atoms were gamboling before my eyes. This time the smaller groups kept modestly in the background. My mental eye, tendered more acute by repeated visions of the kind, could now distinguish larger structures, of manifold conformation:

long rows, sometimes more closely fitted together; all twining and twisting in snake-like motion. But look! What was that? One of the snakes had seized hold of its own tail, and the form whirled mockingly before my eyes. As if by a flash of lightning I awoke; and this time also I spent the rest of the night working on the consequences of the hypothesis[67].

Based on insight provided from this dream, Kekulé postulated that instead of forming a single chain as it does in the alkanes, carbon atoms in benzene are arranged in rings. This major conceptual breakthrough, which marked the birth of organic chemistry, arose, not through pure logic, but through a dream.

SCIENTIFIC PARADIGMS. Another example indicating that science is not strictly a rational endeavor is the existence of scientific paradigms. A paradigm is the milieu of conventions, premises, and assumptions that govern the types of experiments that are conducted in any field of science[68]. Paradigms are present in all fields of science and occur on all levels. The history of each field of science follows a very similar pattern. In pre-modern science, investigators had to formulate their own view of how the system they were studying operated. Eventually a major scientist came along who combined the earlier work into a unifying paradigm that would control the questions and experiments that later workers used. After a while, clues appeared suggesting that the paradigm didn't perfectly describe nature. At first, scientists ignored these clues because, despite flaws, the current theory still did a pretty good job describing most of the data. However, as more and more data were built up that didn't fit the theory, a scientist appeared who looked at the assembled facts in a different way that produced a new theory. The introduction of the new theory is called a scientific revolution, or paradigm shift, because the new paradigm could incorporate several aspects of nature that the previous paradigm had ignored. A new paradigm in a scientific discipline usually leads to major new insights into that discipline, because the paradigm leads to a whole new set of questions that could not have been even asked under the old paradigm.

Because paradigms control, both consciously and unconsciously, how scientists view their discipline, they also determine the nature of the experiments that scientists conduct. Scientific paradigms are powerful because they focus scientific experiments on testing or enlarging the aspects of the natural world to which the paradigm may be applied. However, this strength is also a weakness, because it is impossible for a scientist to think of experiments that lie outside of the paradigm.

METAPHYSICS OF SCIENCE. A major problem with discussing the metaphysics of science is the fact that the terminology of metaphysics is incredibly fuzzy. Four terms have commonly been used to mean the same thing, materialism, scientific materialism, scientism, and naturalism (see Fig. 2).

Physical phenomenona have natural causes	The physical dimension is all there is			
Methodological naturalism	Ontological naturalism	Materialism	Scientific Materialism	The scientific method is the only way to solve problems
				Scientism

Figure 2: *Chart showing how the metaphysical terms relating to the nature of reality are related.*

Materialism and *scientific materialism*: As noted earlier in this book, materialism is the theory that only the physical world is real. According to materialism, if you cannot see, feel, sense, or measure something then it simply doesn't exist. Scientific materialism is a term that means essentially the same thing, that the material universe that science studies is all that there is.

Scientism implies that the only viable way to study reality is through the scientific method. Obviously, because science can only study objects one can see, sense, or measure, scientism is built upon a materialist basis, but in scientism, materialism is more implied than stated.

Naturalism is a term that has a wide range of meanings. It can be used as a synonym for materialism, but it can also be used to imply that the natural world exists and is a valid subject for study. To help clear up this uncertainty, Robert Pennock distinguished *methodological naturalism* from *ontological naturalism*[69]. Methodological naturalism means that there is a natural explanation to all phenomena. Ontological naturalism implies that the physical world is all that there is, which is of course the premise of materialism.

To make the terminology in this book as clear as possible, I will use only two terms: *materialism* and *naturalism*. When I want to talk about the theory that the material world is all there is, I will use "materialism"; I will not use "scientific materialism". Although much of this book discusses the weaknesses in the assumptions of scientism, I will use the term in only a limited way. When I use "naturalism", I will mean methodological naturalism; I will not use naturalism in an ontological sense. I do this because it is important to distinguish between the concept that there is a natural explanation for all physical phenomena, which carries no implication about whether or not there is a spiritual dimension, and the concept that the natural world is all there is.

As noted earlier in the chapter, science has many hidden premises, one of the most important of which is naturalism. Science, of course. cannot exist without a naturalist view of reality. Clearly, if everything in the world, such as lightning, happened because some gods were angry, there would be no need to find an explanation for how and why physical phenomena happen. Not only that, if phenomena were merely a product of angry gods, they would not have a consistent pattern that could yield answers if studied.

One of the key misunderstandings that materialists make is that they assume that the overwhelming success science has had over the centuries implies that materialism is a compelling world-view. Another way to say this is that they confuse methodological naturalism, which is crucial to the operation of science, with ontological naturalism, which is not. Over the past 500 years or so, science has slowly demystified the phenomenal world; educated people no longer believe that lightning, thunder, earthquakes, tsunamis, volcanic eruptions, or any other dramatic physical occurrences are products of angry gods. However, this doesn't mean that the world of our thoughts, creativity, insights, emotions, is invalid because none of them can be measured by scientific techniques. The world's wisdom traditions recognize that these ineffable aspects of our experience are manifestation of the spiritual dimension. In contrast materialists would dismiss these experiences as being simply epiphenomena produced by reactions in our brains.

THE FALLACIES IN MATERIALIST REASONING ON SCIENCE - SUMMARY

The materialists' view that science produces certainty in the knowledge of the world, whereas spiritual practice does not, is obviously based upon misconception of what science can say about the world. As noted above, there are several areas where the materialist view of science is simply wrong. First off, the practice of science is not totally rational. It involves considerable input from intuition and creativity, aspects of the mind that, according to skeptics, are not to be trusted because they arise from chemical or electrical reactions in one's brain. Secondly, paradigm shifts occur at all levels in each discipline of science, which means that science is continually evolving. I have been a geologist for nearly 60 years and can attest that even a supposedly rock-solid science like geology has evolved dramatically in those years. Many of the "facts" I learned about geology in my under-graduate courses in the 1960s have long since been discarded and I am certain that the "facts" that students are learning today will be equally outdated fifty years hence. In other words, there is no "unshakable truth" in science. Finally, although it is true that science is rooted in naturalism, making the jump from the methodological naturalism of science to materialism, a step the materialists make without hesitation, is an intellectual leap that is totally invalid.

SCIENCE AND MAYA

How do views of the mystics, who say that all is *maya*, illusion, fit into the solid world of science. After all, as noted in the beginning of this book, this is one reason I participated in the Three-Year Retreat. In my experience, it comes down to how we view and define reality. One of my insights from the Three-Year Retreat was to recognize "appearance emptiness", and to realize that our experiences are filtered through our concepts of reality. The goal of a mystic is to remain, as much as possible, in the realization of "appearance emptiness", whereas most of us reside in the world of concepts. The world of concepts, of course, produces relative reality, whereas the world of appear-ance emptiness is the world of Ultimate Reality. There is nothing wrong with concepts per se. If you interpret what you see outside to indicate that it is raining (which is a concept) then everyone who goes outside without an umbrella or raincoat, regardless of whether they are a mystic or a materialist, is going to get wet. The concepts inherent in science are more complex than merely saying that it is raining, because they may change as paradigms shift, however they have given us a wealth of handy things, such as cars, airplanes, and computers.

Mystics consider relative reality to be illusory because it does not acquaint us with the true nature of reality, which is beyond all concepts. The fact that Eastern religions consider relative reality as illusory doesn't mean that it is not real, that it is "make believe", or that it cannot be a fruitful realm for study. It is an internally consistent realm where all the scientific constants, such as the atomic weights of the elements, the force of gravity, or the speed of light are valid. The illusion arises when we develop the belief that what we see in relative reality is all that exists in the world. Mystics would say that there is a whole world of Ultimate Reality, which we can access through spiritual practices, that lies beyond the world of relative reality. Furthermore, mystics would say that the insights we derive from our interactions with Ultimate Reality are much more valuable than all the goodies that science has brought us through relative reality.

Relative reality is also considered illusory by Buddhists, because, by their definition, "real" is something that is changeless. This definition means that, to Buddhists, only the spiritual dimension is real. Everything in the physical world changes, although for some features the change happens so slowly that we cannot experience it. Even mountains as dramatic as the Teton Range are temporary. The Tetons were not there 10 million years ago and 10 million years from now they will have been eroded away to mere stumps of their present forms — those 20 million represent only a minute fraction of the 4.5 billion-year history of the Earth. Because every physical thing is changing, the physical world is not "real" by the Buddhist definition. Hence to Buddhist and Hindu mystics, the solidity of the world around us is illusory, which is another reason why Buddhists refer to the physical world as relative reality.

SCIENCE AND LINEAR THINKING

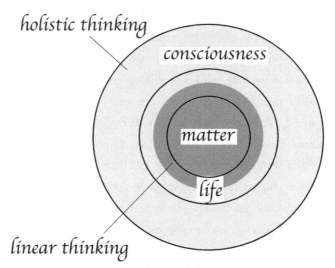

Figure 3. *Diagram showing how the domains of linear and holistic thinking are related within the reality as viewed by spiritual people (i.e. Figure 1. B).*

One feature that makes science and religion different is the way that the two disciplines look at the world. As noted in the previous chapter, science relies on linear thinking. This is not a bad thing because, without linear thinking, no progress could be made in science at all. The scientific method outlined above is a very specific process of setting up theories and setting up experiments that can test them. Religion, in contrast, is dependent on holistic thinking, without which the literature about the mystical insights that make up the core of religion cannot be properly understood. This means that, because they think about reality differently, science and religion cannot be in conflict. Instead, as noted by many authors, they are complementary ways of experiencing reality. Of course, they cannot be entirely complementary because science, with its linear thinking, can study only the physical world, whereas religion is concerned with the spiritual dimension that penetrates the physical realm. Science, therefore, covers a much smaller domain than does religion (Fig. 3).

CHAPTER 5

Neurotheology

INTRODUCTION – A DEFINITION
OF NEUROTHEOLOGY

In the past decades a considerable amount of research has been
done on how the human brain responds to spiritual experiences.
This field has been given the name *neurotheology*[70]. Many atheists
use arguments from the field of neurotheology to dismiss the
importance of the religious experience. To understand the basis
of the atheists' arguments, this chapter delves into the field of
neurotheology. Neurotheology has been broadly defined as the
study of the interaction between religious experiences and the
human brain:

> Neurotheology refers to the field of study linking
> the neurosciences with theology... However,

neurotheology is, in some sense, a misnomer since it should actually refer to the totality of religion and the religious experience as well as theology... Furthermore, since the mind and brain are intimately linked the "neuro" component of neurotheology should be considered to include psychiatry, psychology, cognitive neuroscience, genetics, endocrinology as well as other macro- and micro-perspectives of the neurosciences[71].

To understand the concepts of neurotheology, this chapter will first discuss the nature of the brain. Then it will consider the discipline of neurotheology in detail.

THE STRUCTURE OF THE BRAIN

The human brain consists of three major parts—the brain stem, the cerebellum, and the cerebrum (Fig. 4A), which, generally, reflect the presumed development of the brain during the evolution from reptiles to mammals and humans. At the top of the spinal cord and the base of the brain is the brain stem, which is the most primitive portion of the brain. The brain stem regulates important functions that seem to lie outside of our conscious control, such as heart rate and respiration. Above the brain stem is the cerebellum, which controls balance, coordination, and sensorimotor relationships.

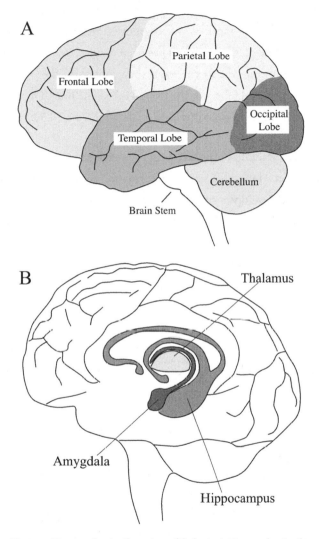

Figure 4. *Diagrams showing the anatomy of the brain. A. Diagram showing the brain stem, cerebellum, and the various lobes of the cerebrum. B. Diagram showing the limbic system that lies deep in the left temporal lobe. A similar arrangement is found in the right lobe. Diagrams modified from figures supplied by Shuttershock.com.*

Above the cerebellum and brain stem is the cerebrum, which is responsible for most of our cognitive functions. The convolute structure of the cerebrum has been divided into four major lobes. From the rear to the front they consist of the occipital lobe, the parietal lobe and the frontal lobe. The fourth lobe, the temporal lobe, lies on either side of the brain (Fig. 4A).

The occipital lobe houses the primary visual center of the brain. The parietal lobe takes sensory information from all parts of the brain and develops a spatial sense of self. It is involved in most operations of orienting the body to the world, including social interactions. The major lobe of the brain is the frontal lobe; it is in control of what are known as the executive functions: the ability to concentrate, to make plans, to initiate actions, and to regulate emotional responses. The frontal lobe is also involved in the senses of smell and taste. The lower parts of the temporal lobes take input from the visual portions of occipital lobe to construct the way we typically view the world. The upper parts of the temporal lobes are involved with language and hearing.

The cerebrum is split from front to back into two hemispheres by a deep fissure. The hemispheres are connected by a wide band of fibers known as the corpus callosum. The structures of the two hemispheres are similar; each hemisphere controls the opposite side of the body. Traditionally the left hemisphere is considered to be associated with analytical and quantitative thought, in contrast to the right hemisphere, which is associated with the creative and holistic aspects of thought. Recent studies using brain imaging indicate that the asymmetry of brain function is more complex than this[72], but, as will be seen later in this chapter, there is strong evidence from people who have had a stroke that damages the left hemisphere of the brain affects one's tendency to view reality in a purely rational way.

Along with these obvious features, the brain also contains the limbic system, a number of important features that are in charge of emotion and which lie deep within the brain adjacent to the temporal lobes (Fig. 4B). Because most of our experiences are overlain (or underlain) by emotions, the limbic system is closely interconnected with the rest of the brain. Key among the features of the limbic system are the amygdala, hippocampus, and the thalamus. Each hemisphere of the brain has an amygdala and a hippocampus. The amygdala is named for its almond-like shape and lies deep within the temporal lobes on either side of the brain. The amygdala plays an important role in how we process emotion and memory. The hippocampus, which is named after the Greek word for seahorse, which is what its shape evokes, plays an important role in helping the brain to convert short-term memory into long-term memory. It also helps form spatial memory, which is critical with how one navigates the world. The thalamus is connected to many different functions in the brain, including sensory, motor and language systems. It is functionally connected to the hippocampus and seems to help with memory and spatial relations.

HOW RELIGIOUS PRACTICE
AFFECTS THE BRAIN

Over the past thirty years, neurological studies have suggested that religious practices may produce responses in various portions of the brain. These studies have included imaging patients while they are conducting various religious practices, the study of effect of brain surgery on patients, and studies of patients who show various neurological problems such as epilepsy or psychosis. Results of these studies vary. Together they suggest that the areas of the brain that appear to be involved in religious experiences include the temporal lobe, the frontal lobe, the parietal lobe, the limbic system, the autonomic nervous system, or a combination of areas in the brain[73].

THE TEMPORAL LOBE: Perhaps the most popular explanation for the religious experience is that it is related to electrical discharges in the temporal lobe[74]. A major reason for this conclusion is that some people with temporal lobe epilepsy evince a heightened sense of spirituality[75]. Several authors have presented cases of modern patients who had undergone spiritual experiences and who also had temporal lobe epilepsy[76]. This has led some authors to conclude that most religious figures in history were epileptic[77], although, obviously, clinical evidence for this conclusion is totally lacking.

Other evidence that the temporal lobe is a site of religious experience comes from the fact that stimulation of the temporal lobe can produce intense hallucinations[78]. In addition, experiments have suggested that electrical impulses to the temporal lobe tend to produce spiritual experiences such as the sense of a presence, although it must be pointed out that the results of those experiments have been questioned because they could not be duplicated[79]. These findings have led many authors to presume that the temporal lobe is the site of the God experience, i.e., it is the God center[80].

FRONTAL LOBES: When the brain is resting and not concentrating on anything, the major brain activity lies in a circuit between the prefrontal cortex, the foremost part of the frontal lobe, and the postcingulate cortex, which is considered part of the limbic system. This circuit has been called the "default mode" network[81]. When a person's mind is not concentrated on a project, the default mode takes over and the mind wanders around with questions and thoughts about ourselves, our problems, our hopes, and our expectations. Meditation involves paying attention to all the sensations arising in our bodies, from the sense of breathing, to the subtle feelings throughout the body, to the arising of thoughts. Focusing attention on these sensations activate areas in the prefrontal cortex. The enhanced activity in the prefrontal lobe calms the default mode and shuts down the wandering, daydreaming mind. In seasoned contemplatives, this change is seen to persist even when they are not meditating[82], results that suggest that religious practice enhances areas of the frontal lobe.

PARIETAL LOBE: The superior parietal lobe plays an important role in self orientation. Because religious practice tends to weaken one's sense of self, it is logical to presume that religious practice affects the parietal lobe. There is some clinical evidence for this. Patients who have had malignant tumors surgically removed from portions of the parietal lobe report enhanced feelings of self-transcendence (ST):

> In conclusion, our symptom-lesion mapping study demonstrates a causative link between brain functioning and ST. In particular, the study shows that damage to the posterior parietal areas may induce unusually fast changes of a stable personality dimension related to transcendental self-referential awareness. Thus, dysfunctional parietal neural activity may underpin altered spiritual and religious attitudes and behaviors[83].

These findings suggest that religious experience is associated with lowering activity in the parietal lobe.

THE LIMBIC SYSTEM. The suggestion that the religious experience arises from the limbic system is based upon two arguments. One is that the key qualities of the religious experience are that it is ineffable and noetic. Because the limbic system integrates stimuli with internal experiences, and is a part of a neural network that marks experience with positive or negative emotions, it is reasonable to assume that the limbic system plays an important role in the religious experience, as indicated by the following quote:

> Available evidence, however, suggests that mesolimbic structures, the hippocampus and especially the amygdala, are likely the critical

generators of a feeling of unreality about the self or external reality[84].

The second argument is based on the fact that religious practice enhances a person's sense of empathy. Because empathy is developed in the limbic system, it is reasonable to assume that the limbic system is involved in religious practice. As one investigator says:

> Empathy arises from circuitry involving the insula[85] and the amygdala. Brain imaging indicates that people who engaged in loving-kindness meditation showed increase in the right amygdala's activity when shown photos of suffering[86].

THE AUTONOMIC NERVOUS SYSTEM. The autonomic nervous system is part of the nervous system that acts unconsciously and regulates bodily functions, including heart rate, digestion, and breathing. Many studies have shown that meditation can lower blood pressure, heart rate and metabolism. Clearly this means that the autonomic nervous system is involved in the practice.

INTEGRATED PROCESSES ACROSS THE BRAIN. Some studies indicate that the religious experience is spread across several, or many areas of the brain. For example, as noted above, meditation activates parts of the frontal lobe, which calms the default mode, a circuit that involves both the frontal lobe and the limbic system. In addition, brain image studies of religious folk who are reading the Bible indicate that the experience involves the frontal and parietal lobes[87]. Because brain imaging studies have increasingly shown that other experiences are spread across the brain, it is reasonable to expect that the religious experience would be also. As noted by Shukla and colleagues:

> What we found to be common in a majority of the studies that "no single God spot exists"…. There is no single anatomic site which can be dubbed as overtly religious or spiritualistic than the other. They all work in unison and each one is special in its own unique way…[88]

CRITICISMS OF NEUROTHEOLOGY

The field of neurotheology, although blossoming, is hardly free of controversy[89]. There are three arguments against neurotheology: First there are criticisms of the nature of the experiments, both with respect to the instrumentation and the way that patients were chosen. Second notes that, even if one can localize the portion of the brain that responds to religious experience, it in no way explains the qualia of that experience. Third is the contention that ascribing experiences to discrete locations in the brain is fallacious.

EXPERIMENTAL PROBLEMS. Obviously obtaining images of the brains for people who are undergoing subjective experiences is fraught with problems. One of the major problems is that the spiritual experience in a lab setting is hardly the same experience that may arise spontaneously[90], and thus it is hard to extrapolate between the two. Furthermore, because the experience is highly subjective, an experiment involving many subjects is likely to be imaging a wide and unquantifiable range of experiences[91]. All of this adds a huge and indeterminate uncertainty to the whole field of neurotheology.

WHAT DO THE BRAIN IMAGES MEAN? One major implication of neurotheology is that the heightened neurological activity seen in the brains of people experiencing religious experience actually cause that experience[92]. Although many investigators do not say this outright, this subtle form of materialism within neurotheology is seen as a major problem by many critics of the field[93]. Part of this problem arises because, as noted in chapter three, all major religions acknowledge that there is both an immanent and transcendent nature to the spiritual dimension. The immanent aspect describes the effect that religious practice has on the human personality, and this may be reflected in changes in the way the brain operates. The changes in the brain function between experienced contemplatives and those who don't practice prayer or meditation may be recording the immanent aspect of spirituality.

The situation is very different, however, if one is trying to interpret the brain images in terms of the transcendent aspect of the spiritual experience. Are the areas of the brain that light up in images of people undergoing a religious experience the source of that experience or are they a product of that experience? In other words is the religious experience simply a product of electrical discharges in the brain or is there much more to them? That is a question that is impossible for science to answer.

THE PROBLEM WITH BRAIN GEOGRAPHY. Perhaps the biggest problem with neurotheology and with cognitive science in general, comes from the assumption that distinct brain functions can be located in discrete regions of the brain. This assumption is made although:

> ...cognitive neuroscientists will acknowledge that the brain is a dynamic, functionally integrated, and highly interdependent system of complex synaptic-neural networks that interact in non-linear ways[94].

Since it is true that the brain is a highly integrated system, it is difficult to argue that any experience is restricted or located in any given area of the brain. As pointed out by one set of neuroscientists:

> What we found to be common in a majority of the studies was that "no single God spot exists". The brain is a hard wired center of neurons in the seas of gray and white matter...There is no single anatomical site which can be dubbed as overly religious or spiritualistic than the other[95].

Another problem with the concept that the neural response to experiences is located within isolated areas of the brain is the concept of neuroplasticity. Until the late twentieth century it was assumed that after the brain formed through young adulthood, it remained static until a person died. It is now recognized that the brain can grow throughout the life of an individual, a process called neuroplasticity. Neuroplasticity can form at all levels from regrowth of individual synapses to remapping of cortical zones after an injury[96]. The existence of neuroplasticity explains why a number of medical anomalies exist, such as a small number of children with 90% of their cranium filled with cerebral-spinal fluid (i.e. with only 10% of a normal brain) who have I.Q.s of 100[97], or why some individuals with no cognitive impairment have brains that show, on autopsy, evidence of plaque, neurofibrillary tangles and other degenerative features indicative of Alzheimer's disease[98]. If the brain can be so plastic, then it is unreasonable to assume that the neural response to experiences would be fixed in only one location.

Important evidence in the non-localization of the religious experience comes from a spellbinding book, *My Stroke of Insight*. In it, the author, Dr. Jill Taylor writes about the massive stroke that she suffered in December of 1996. Dr. Taylor is a brain scientist, and she knew exactly what was happening as the stroke progressed. A blood vessel had ruptured in the left side of her brain and the pooling blood was slowly destroying the neurons that occupied her left brain. She observed that, as the stroke progressed, she slowly lost her language and cognitive abilities. In response to this, she slipped into a sense of peace. As she says:

> In the absence of my left hemisphere's analytical judgement, I was completely entranced by the feelings of tranquility, safety, blessedness, euphoria, and omniscience[99].

After the bleeding had been stabilized, her body felt like a lump. She could not determine where it began or where it ended, she couldn't hear or say anything, and could barely move parts of her body. Her analytical mind was no longer available to record and relate to the outside world. After eight years of hard work, Dr. Taylor was able to recover her cognitive abilities, but even after she had recovered, the insights she had attained during the stroke stayed with her.

> Based upon my experience of losing my left mind, I whole-heartedly believe that the feeling of deep inner peace is neurological circuitry located in our right brain. This circuitry is constantly running and always available for us to hook into. The feeling of peace is something that happens in the present moment. It's not something that we bring with us from the past or project into the future. Step one to experiencing inner peace is the willingness to be present in the right here, right now[100].

A similar thing happened to Ram Dass, who had a stroke in 1997 and, like Dr. Taylor, he originally lost his ability to speak. Afterward as he says:

> I've noticed something interesting: when there is not such a rush of words the imagery gets subtler.... With the left brain—the verbal, analytical half— less dominant since the stroke, maybe the right is just freer to come out and play[101].

The experiences described by Dr. Taylor and Ram Dass have two important implications toward the field of neurotheology. First, it indicates that the religious experience is likely to be a function that is inherent in the brain, and that it is simply obscured by constant mental chatter that dominates the function of our brains. Dr. Taylor and, to a lesser extent, Ram Dass, obtained access to this insight because their strokes had destroyed, or lessened the constant chatter that dominated their brains. This, of course, sounds exactly like what the teachings of the world's religions tell us. To gain access to the divine, one has to eliminate the fog of ego that fills one's brain, which is obscuring the spiritual world that surrounds us. Most of the religious practices are designed to do just this (see chapter eight). Second, it indicates that the neurological effect of spiritual experiences is not one of addition, but one of subtraction. By this, I mean that, rather than being a random electrical discharge that adds some extra input to a person's brain, the religious experience could be caused by impulses in the brain that reduce the intensity of the ego.

CONCLUSIONS

Considering all the problems with neurotheology, is it really a valid field of science? My answer would be "yes" for three reasons. First, to a large extent, most of the criticisms about neurotheology discussed above do not negate the importance of this field of study, they merely indicate the huge problems facing investigators in this field. These problems are well known to the major scientists working in neurotheology[102]. For example,

Davidson admits to the problem of experimental rigor in that, while compiling research results for the neurological effects of loving-kindness meditation, he found that only 3% of the studies were rigorous enough to be acceptable[103]. Similarly, the problem of interpreting exactly what the brain images of religious experience mean is also recognized by the practitioners of neurotheology as indicated by this quote (italics were in the original quote):

> The results do not suggest either that the brain activity *caused* the experience to occur or whether the findings reflected the brain's *response* to the experience...[104]

The second reason why neurotheology is valid is because, despite the many problems involved in interpreting its results, it helps explain observations that have long been made about how religious practice changes people's minds. For example, it is known that people who have engaged in abundant contemplative practice tend to be less prone to emotional upheaval than those who do not. The recognition, noted above, that meditation quiets the "default mode" in the brain helps one to understand why this happens. It is possible, therefore, that brain studies can eventually lead to the understanding of metanoia, the process whereby religious practice changes a person's view of the world.

The third, and perhaps the most important, reason is that neurotheology is one field where science and religion cooperate to solve problems of common interest. As noted by Barbour, there are four ways in which science and religion may interact: 1) through conflict, 2) through mutual independence, 3) through dialogue, and 4) through integration[105]. Neurotheology is one field where science and religion may interact through integration. As noted by Newberg,

> ...neurotheology...might also be viewed as a nexus in which those from the religious as well as a scientific side can come together to explore deep issues about humanity in a constructive and complementary manner[106].

Although it is unlikely that neurotheology will ever be able to shed light on the transcendent aspects of the religious experience, the fact that it may help us understand the immanent aspect of the spiritual dimension makes it a very valid undertaking.

CHAPTER 6

The Atheists' View of the Religious Experience

As I argued in the previous chapters, spiritual beliefs arise in response to the religious experience, therefore religious faith is not so much rooted in a belief as in an experience. As has already been noted, this experience is not rare; in a 2009 survey the Pew Forum on Religion in Public life reported that 49% of Americans report having had a religious or mystical experience. The widespread occurrence of the religious experience is clearly a problem that atheists need to explain, since they are trying to convince people that there is no spiritual dimension in life. One would expect that books by atheists would spend a lot of time arguing about the nature of the religious experience.

Many authors, such as Hitchens and Dennett don't mention it at all, others such as Harris and Dawkins, simply give it a short dismissal[107]. This is partially because, in the materialist view, consciousness is merely an epiphenomenon of neural activity in the brain and not much more needs to be said. The atheists consider the spiritual experience to be a meaningless mental discharge within the brain of a person who is somehow childish enough to think it is important.

Atheists use four classes of arguments to reason away the existence of the spiritual experience. Some of the arguments use sophisticated applications of neurotheology; others are not so closely tied to science. Listed below, from the most ridiculous to the most sophisticated, these arguments are:

1.   People who report religious experiences are childish folk who don't understand the value of pure reason.

2.   Consciousness is merely an epiphenomenon produced by the reactions in the brain and carries no significance whatsoever. Since the religious experience is a manifestation of consciousness, it too has no significance.

3.   The religious experience is simply a form of psychosis.

4.   The religious experience is the result of a transient discharge of the temporal lobe of

the brain and, thus, it is a natural phenomenon with no spiritual significance.

PEOPLE WHO BELIEVE THEIR SPIRITUAL EXPERIENCE IS REAL ARE CHILDISH

It is common for atheists to dismiss the validity of the spiritual experience by using arguments that carry a tone that belittles those who consider the experience to be valid. A good example is:

> Like the child who feels her wishes control and interact with the parents' behaviors, the convinced adult concludes that somehow her thoughts interact with God. Somehow through the vast unknowns of time and space, God acts through the trivial nuances of human thinking. The absolute stupidity of the compulsion is not seen[108].

In addition to accusing spiritual people of being childish, atheists, because they consider linear thinking to be the only valid way of viewing the world, commonly accuse spiritual people of weak and sloppy thinking. The quote below is a good example (italics are in the original quote):

> Egocentrism is not necessarily correlated with arrogance and extroversion. Quite humble people can be just as egocentric as the most abrasive braggart. *Egocentrism* refers to the relative reliance placed on one's experience as proof of reality…. The ludicrous nature of this type of magical

thinking is most apparent in the God Experience. Ultimately, as the final source of proof, the person relies on personal experience (his or her thoughts) to defend the validity of the event. In one form or another, the person contends that God has interacted with his or her *thoughts.* Yet, there is no physical evidence[109].

The above quote carries a bizarre definition of egotism, because as I have noted earlier, spiritual experiences are commonly associated with a decrease in the intensity with which one addresses his or her ego. The argument is also ludicrous because it should be obvious to everyone that nobody can know anything except through personal experience. The atheist who wrote this obviously assumes that his experience gleaned from rational thought is valid mainly because it is *his* experience and that the trans-rational experiences of others are childish because they are not derived through logic. Obviously, because thoughts are entirely mental processes, there is no physical evidence for either spiritual or rational thoughts.

THE RELIGIOUS EXPERIENCE IS A PRODUCT OF CHEMICAL (OR ELECTRICAL) REACTIONS IN THE BRAIN

As noted in chapter one, a major argument some atheists use is that your thoughts are merely an epiphenomenon of your brain. All your experiences, your consciousness, and even your concept of "me" are constructed by chemical or electrical reactions in your brain; they have no reality apart from that. In addition, these materialists argue that, because your brain has been conditioned by evolution to seek patterns in the world around you, you will append meaning to a random pattern, even when none is there[110]. In other words, the religious experience is a meaningless electronic discharge in your brain to which you ascribe an irrelevant importance. Talking about your religious experience:

> Maybe it is a combination of an environmental stressor plus an anomalous brain hiccup—random neural firings, for example, or perhaps a minor temporal lobe seizure, the latter of which are well documented as causing both auditory and visual hallucinations along with hyper-religious behavior[111].

The argument that your religious experience is simply a meaningless discharge in your brain suffers from the problem that it doesn't specify where the meaninglessness of mental phenomena stops. Obviously, if the materialistic view of consciousness is valid, then the thoughts of these materialists are also produced by chemical reactions in their brains. How is it that their experiences are meaningful, whereas mine are not? One could read their argument like this: "Your religious experiences are simply meaningless electrical discharges in your brain. In contrast, the electrical discharges in my brain, which produce a coherent, materialistic view of reality, actuality present a meaningful, understandable experience."

If you logically follow the argument that mental events are simply chemical reactions in the brain, then you are forced into profound nihilism, which implies that everything in our lives is meaningless. In other words, according to this view, the arguments of atheists that the spiritual experience is simply a meaningless electrical reaction in a religious person's brain is itself the product of an equally meaningless electrical reaction in an atheist's brain.

RELIGIOUS EXPERIENCE IS A TYPE OF PSYCHOSIS

One argument neoatheists use to discount the significance of the religious experience is that it is a type of psychosis[112]. Here is the typical argument that has appeared in several books:

> Many people believe in God because they have seen a vision of him—or of an angel or a virgin in blue—with their own eyes. This argument from personal experience is most convincing to those who have had one. But it is the least convincing to anyone else, and anyone knowledgeable about psychology. You say you have experienced God directly? Well, some people have experienced a pink elephant, but that probably doesn't impress you... Individuals in asylums think they are Napoleon or Charlie Chaplin, or that the entire world is conspiring against them, or that they can broadcast their thoughts into other people's heads. We humor them but don't take their internally revealed beliefs seriously, mostly because not many people share them. Religious experiences

differ only in that the people who experience them are numerous[113].

This argument is subject to three major problems. First is it trying to compare the experiences of sane people with those who are insane. The founders of the great religions, particularly Saint Paul and Muhammad had profound religious experiences, but clearly were not insane. They were able to attract people to their movement and develop complex religious organizations that have persisted for thousands of years. This is certainly not something a psychotic person could do.

The second problem is that the reasoning involved is a classic example of a false syllogism. A syllogism is a logical argument that is key to deductive reasoning. An example of a syllogism is:

Humans have two legs
Socrates is human
Therefore, Socrates has two legs

The first two lines are premises, the first premise gives the property of a class (i.e. humans). The second premise notes that Socrates is a member of that class. The third line is a conclusion that, since Socrates is a human, he has to share the same property as other humans (i.e. he has two legs).

We can reconstruct the quote above about religion being a psychosis into the following syllogism:

> Psychotic people have visions
> Religious people have visions
> Therefore, religious people are psychotic

The first premise gives a property of a class (psychotic people), whereas the second premise gives a property of another class (religious people). The conclusion, namely that because religious people share the same property as psychotic people, they, too, must be psychotic, is not logically defendable. Just because two groups share the same property it does not mean that they must be part of the same, larger, group. A good example of this faulty logic is this syllogism

> Crows have two legs
> Socrates has two legs
> Therefore, Socrates is a crow

The final problem with this kind of reasoning is that it, like many of the arguments atheists use, it is an insidious way to approach a discussion. As with the quotes cited at the beginning of this chapter, this argument demeans those people who view the world based upon a religious experience. By implying that religious people are in some way psychotic, the author of the above passage does not have to address the gist of the arguments that people of faith put forth about the validity of religion. Rather, he simply implies that they are invalid because the people who make them are insane.

THE RELIGIOUS EXPERIENCE IS DUE TO A DISCHARGE IN "GOD CENTER" OF THE BRAIN

There are several explanations that ascribe the origin of the religious experience to transient electrical discharges in the God Center of the brain, which many authors place in the temporal lobe.

> Instead, my hypothesis is that the God Experience is a phenomenon that is associated with the construction of the temporal lobe[114].

As noted in the previous chapter, this model, which avers that the religious experience simply an electrical discharge in the temporal lobe, also contends that it evolved as a way to mollify the angst of humans[115]. This view of how the religious experience arises leads to an argument like this:

> How do you know that your religious experience is not a simple trick of your brain—the unfolding of a perfectly natural temporal lobe transient? How can you trust such an experience when, through science, we can convincingly mimic the face of God[116]?

The most extreme of these explanations is that the religious experience is caused by epileptic seizures in the temporal lobe of the brain. As noted in the previous chapter, people have long associated epilepsy with religious sensitivity; as early as the eighth century the Christian world interpreted Muhammad's visions as epileptic seizures[117]. Modern authors have argued that temporal lobe seizures are particularly effective in inducing the religious experience. In fact, some authors go far enough in this argument to maintain that most of the religious figures in the past were epileptic[118].

As noted in the previous chapters, detailed studies on this problem affirm that there is no correlation between spirituality and epilepsy[119]. As one investigator wrote:

> One potential drawback of this model is that most individuals with seizures tend to have repeated seizures with relatively similar types of symptoms. Since most strong spiritual experiences occur only once or a few times in an individual's life, the possibility that they are somehow related to spontaneous seizure activity seems less likely[120].

The problem with all these arguments about the God Center in the brain is that they grossly oversimply the field of neurotheology. As noted in the previous chapter, there is ample evidence from recent studies of neurotheology which show that, because the brain is a highly integrated system, religious experiences are distributed across the brain and there is no "God Center". The assumption that the God Center exists is simply sloppy science.

CONCLUSION

True, there are some very good reasons to assume that your mental experiences come from your brain. People with brain damage caused by accident, stroke, or Alzheimer's disease show varying degrees of disability ranging from aphasia to complete unconsciousness. Rather than *assuming* that all consciousness is produced in the brain, the mystical view of reality contends that some aspect of consciousness is derived from outside the brain. In other words, rather than the brain being merely a producer of consciousness, as implied by materialists, religious people maintain that it is also a receiver of consciousness. A good analogy for this receiver might be the old-fashioned TV set (modern TV sets have printed circuits that rarely fail):

> If one of the circuits in your TV malfunctions, the TV reception will suffer in a way that is very similar to a person with brain damage. The TV image might be jittery and fuzzy, or there might be no image at all. However, just because you can tie the cause of the bad reception to problems in the TV circuitry, you certainly wouldn't maintain that the TV show was produced within your TV set. Equating neurophysiology to the study of consciousness is equivalent to looking at the activities of the circuits in the back of the TV to determine whether the show being projected on the screen is *Hamlet* or *Gilligan's Island.* To be more extreme, to maintain that we understand the source of consciousness because we understand

> where the brain responds to stimuli is like looking
> in the back to the TV set to determine from what
> city the TV show is being broadcast[121].

All religions contend that the religious experience is always there; it is simply obscured by our continual mental chatter. They believe that once you drop the sense of self, Ultimate Reality reveals itself to you. As noted in the previous chapter, there is no way atheists can prove the stimulation of a part of the brain *produces* transcendent experiences rather than simply *opens* one to them.

Although atheists belittle the religious experience, some of them say that they will believe in God when you can prove to them that He exists. When they make this comment, they are talking as if the belief in God is similar to some scientific theory that can be argued through logical means. There are two problems with this approach. First, as noted earlier in this book, religion is based upon an experience, it is not a theory that can be argued through reason. Clearly, since atheists believe that the religious experience is merely a malfunction of a person's mind, they consider the argument about religion being an experience to be totally invalid. Their attitude is that, if you are mentally unbalanced enough to believe that the experiences in your brain have profound religious meaning, then certainly you are unbalanced enough to ascribe your experiences to God.

The second problem with all of the arguments used to dismiss religious experiences is that, to argue a scientific theory, one has to use linear thinking, wherein a postulate is either true or false.

As argued in the previous chapter, linear thinking does not work well in religion, where holistic thinking is needed to understand the mystical message and the symbolism and metaphor that are used to get the message across. Because materialists are trapped within a world of linear thinking, they cannot conceive that there is another way to understand the nature of reality. As a result they fall into the pre/trans fallacy, which was discussed in chapter three. Since a religious experience cannot be presented in any logical manner, atheists conclude that the person describing a religious experience must be adhering to a pre-rational way of thinking. The possibility that a person may be entirely rational and yet experience a phenomenon that lies *beyond* rationality utterly escapes them.

CHAPTER 7

The Atheists' View of Why Religion Exists

Because atheists believe that the spiritual dimension does not exist, they find that the formation of religions and their persistence through time to be a complete mystery. Religions, their ceremonies and rituals, not to mention the elaborate buildings they occupy, involve such an expenditure of resources, both in time and wealth, that it is difficult for atheists to comprehend how they arose and why they persist. In the words of the famous biologist (and atheist) Richard Dawkins:

> Though the details differ across the world, no known culture lacks some version of the time-consuming, wealth-consuming, hostility-provoking

rituals, the anti-factual, counter-productive fantasies of religion[122].

Because materialists consider that science can answer every question, to them there must be a scientific answer for why religion is present in every culture. Over the past decades, numerous authors have come up with a number of models of how religion began. Most of these models rely on the concept of functionalism, namely that religion evolved because it produced an important function to society. Although these models may be functionalistic, it is clear from the list that follows in this chapter that the proponents of the various theories have different concepts of what this function is. I divide the various models for the origin of religion into two groups: 1) those that are Darwinistic and 2) those that are not:

FORMATION OF RELIGION AS A DARWINISTIC PROCESS

The theories that religion arose as a result of Darwinistic evolution are all examples of cultural evolution. There is a considerable question whether Darwinism can be used to explain the evolution of cultural traits. This is because culture is made up of ideas, not genes. True, Darwinistic evolution involves transfer of information through a population, but the information is coded within the genes of the animals in that population. The pace at which information moves through a population by Darwinistic evolution is dependent on the life span of the individuals. In evolution, the movement of information that takes place is totally passive, those genetic codes that produce creatures that are successful persist for a longer time in the population than those codes that produce creatures that are not successful. In this process the information coded in the genes changes slowly over many generations.

In contrast, cultural evolution involves ideas, and ideas move through populations actively in a way that is nowhere near Darwinistic. Unlike Darwinism, where the transfer of information is entirely passive, the transfer of information in cultural evolution is active. When an idea moves from one person to another, each person choses whether to incorporate that idea unchanged into the category of concepts that person employs every day, or to modify that idea as they incorporate it. Some ideas, such as altruism, compassion, and kindness play an important part in holding a society together, and hence one might use Darwinistic explanations to argue why they persist. Others, such as greed, cruelty, and egotism have a deleterious effect on the cohesion of a society and yet, despite their maladaptive nature, they persist in most societies. Obviously Darwinistic theories cannot explain their persistence, simply because the continuation of these negative traits is far more complex than any functionalist theory can encompass.

As noted above, the argument against the concept that human culture evolved in a Darwinistic manner is that culture is transmitted through human consciousness, and therefore can be modified by any person in the culture. This argument carries no weight with materialists, who consider our minds to be simply chemical reactions in our brains. To them, since humans are products of Darwinian evolution, culture must be as well.

Their question becomes: what pressure or pressures exerted by natural selection favored the impulse that causes people to practice religion? The question gains urgency from standard Darwinian considerations of economy. As noted above, religion is so wasteful, so extravagant; and Darwinian selection habitually targets and eliminates waste[123], so why do religions persist? Several theories have arisen to explain this.

1. **GROUP SELECTION:** In this theory, organized religion arose through an evolutionary process known as group selection. Because religions enhanced the cooperation among people within a group, those groups that followed a religion became more prosperous and successful than those who did not[124]. Thus, over time, religions spread throughout human culture. An obvious problem with this theory is that, if religion provides an advantage to a population of humans, then why are people who affirm a religion so intent on passing it on to others? Such an impulse to help others certainly would not fit with Dawkins' "selfish gene" theory of evolution and would surely decrease any adaptive advantage that religion would impart to a population.

2. **GOD IS THE BIG DADDY:** Another explanation is that religion may not have developed directly through Darwinistic evolution but is a by-product of some other aspects of evolution[125]. One possible explanation is that, because humans have such a long childhood, children have evolved to depend on their parents. With this realization, perhaps religion evolved as a cultural manifestation of this dependence. As Richard Dawkins says:

> Natural selection builds child brains with a
> tendency to believe whatever their parents and
> tribal elders tell them....The inevitable by-product
> is vulnerability to infection by mind viruses[126].

The problem with this theory is that, although children do indeed learn to obey their elders, they also grow up. Growing up involves a process where the children learn the culture of the society and the judgement necessary to make the society work. When people have assimilated that knowledge, they can direct their own children how to behave in a way that fits into the society's norms. Thus, as a child grows up and becomes more sophisticated, the need to obey should disappear and the argument above becomes moot. The insidious implication of Dawkins' theory is that people of religious faith behave that way because they are childish and never grew up. As has been noted elsewhere in this book, arguments such as these, which are contemptuous of religious people, occur frequently in atheist circles.

3. THERE IS A "GOD CENTER" IN THE BRAIN: We have already met this concept in chapter six where materialists argue that the religious experience comes from electrical activity in the temporal lobe or "God Center" of the brain. There are two theories of how the God Center evolved. In one, it evolved as a way to comfort humans as they evolved self-consciousness.

> A biological capacity for the God Experience
> was critical for the survival of the species.
> Without the experiences to balance the terror of
> personal extinction, the existence of the human

phenomenon called the "self" could not be maintained. It would be fragmented by the persistent, gnawing realization that death could come at any time[127].

Another explanation is that it evolved to accommodate Shamanistic healing. Shamanistic healing was one of the major healing techniques available to primitive humans and, according to the proponents of this model, shamanistic healing worked simply because it hypnotized people into feeling that they were cured. Because people who were easily hypnotized had a better rate of survival, a gene evolved that allowed people to be hypnotized by shamans. This "hypnotizability" center in the brain became the "God Center[128]."

As noted in chapter six, the concept that there is a God Center in the brain is a naïve interpretation of the findings of neurotheology, which suggests that the religious experience occurs throughout the brain and that religious insight may be produced by subtraction of distracting aspects of our consciousness, rather than addition of a profound insight. By that I mean that the feelings of tranquility, safety, blessedness, euphoria, and omniscience are always present in one's brain, all one has to do to experience it is to stop the incessant internal chatter about oneself. Although the field of neurotheology has long since dropped the concept of a God Center in the brain, that doesn't keep the idea of a God Center from being a popular concept among atheists.

4. Religion is a Mental Virus: Richard Dawkins postulates that religion is a mental virus that captures people's minds and makes them servants who further propagate this virus, much in a way that a flu virus moves through human communities[129]. In a way this theory is similar to the theory that God is the Big Daddy, given above, whereby childish people, whose brains are conditioned to believe authority become infected with brain viruses. This theory concentrates on the assumption that religion infests "childish" brains. A virus like this has been called a "meme' by Dawkins[130] and childish people are evidently susceptible to infestations of memes. One of the most obvious types of meme is religion.

> Organized religions are organized by people…. But, to reiterate the point I made…that doesn't mean that they were conceived and designed by people….the strong possibility remains that the detailed form of each religion was largely shaped by unconscious evolution. Not by genetic natural selection…. The role of genetic natural selection in the story is to provide the brain, with its predilections and biases — the hardware platform and low-level system software which forms the background for memetic selection[131].

This paragraph implies that, although brains evolved through natural selection, religions have evolved independently as a meme that infects human brains. There are many problems with the theory of memes. The most important of which is the implication, as indicated in the quote above, that memes reproduce in our brains outside of our consciousness. In other words, memetics, the study of how memes reproduce in our brains, involves a totally materialistic view of how the mind works. According to the meme theory, people don't think or make independent concepts, their minds are simply infected by memes, caused by the wholesale replications of what they witness others doing. Memes are considered to be analogous to genes, but, unlike genes, which are distinct material objects, there is no indication of what a meme could be or where it could store its information[132]. Consequently, the term "meme" is poorly defined.

> It seems to me that this word is nothing but an unnecessary synonym of the term "concept"...In neither his definition nor the examples illustrating what memes are does Dawkins mention anything that would distinguish memes from concepts[133].

Apparently, as far as Dawkins is concerned, a meme is distinct from a concept, because, as noted above, memes operate without any conscious participation of the person whose brain a meme has infected.

The idea that religion forms as a result of a "virus" infection in a person's brain is clearly the weakest model that materialists present for the origin of religion. I will leave the evaluation of memes to others[134] and try to explain the argument about religion being a brain virus. In this model, religion forms in the brains of susceptible people through the action of an unspecified virus. This happens without the conscious participation of the "victim". What the virus is, how the infection spreads, and how the virus changes the thought patterns of the victim is never specified. The reader has to take it on faith that this is how religion began, but, of course, atheists are usually disdainful of people who take something on faith.

RELIGION FORMED BY PROCESSES OTHER THAN DARWINISM

Another set of explanations for the origin of religion do not call upon Darwinism. Rather, according to these models, religion has arisen by some sort of mistake or error in human judgement.

5. RELIGION BY COERCION: Organized religion formed from folk religion when the tribal bosses used it to gain power over the masses — i.e. the bosses became appointed (or anointed) by the gods.

> Hawaiian chiefs were typical of chiefs elsewhere, in asserting divinity, divine descent, or at least a hotline to the gods. The chief claimed to serve the people by interceding for them with the gods and reciting ritual formulas to obtain rain, good harvests, and success in fishing....The chief may either combine the offices of political leader and priest in a single person, or may support a separate group of kleptocrats (that is, priests) whose function is to provide ideological justification for the chiefs. That is why chiefdoms devote so much collected tribute to constructing temples and other

public works, which serve as centers of official religion and visible signs of the chief's power[135].

In this model, religion essentially plays a political role in supporting the leaders of a state and practitioners of a religion do so simply to remain in good graces with the society and state. On the surface, this theory appears reasonable because over the past millennia the major empires of the world were supported by religious institutions. This theory is belied, however, by the fact that over the same period of time, monastic communities have also flourished within various religions, where individuals engaged in intense spiritual practice and completely ignored any political activity. Certainly, the model that religion has evolved through coercion cannot explain either monasticism nor mysticism, which, as argued earlier, are the core of many religions.

6. RELIGION IS SIMPLY A MARKET DECISION: Most sociologists maintain that religious decisions are irrational. In contrast, Stark and Finke maintain that people make rational decisions about religion.

> ...we demonstrate that people will accept high religious costs if these result in such high levels of religious benefits that the result is a favorable exchange ratio. That is, people attend not only to cost, but to value in making their decisions[136].

They maintain that the rational decision involved is a market decision in which God or the gods will deliver key benefits — rain, good harvests, and even immortality — in a way that is not available from any other transaction. By their definition (bold type is theirs).

> **RELIGIOUS ORGANIZATIONS** are social enter-
> prises whose primary purpose is to create, main-
> tain, and supply religion to some set of individuals
> and to support and supervise their exchanges with
> a god or gods.

In this model, religions are simply markets where people can buy what they cannot obtain elsewhere — such as a meaning to life or immortality.

The big problem with this model is that it assumes that religion involves only organizations from which one can obtain some sort of spiritual solace. This ignores the fact that many religious people practice outside formal institutions and therefore their practice does not involve any "market" exchange with a religious institution. A good example was the Buddha, who left a comfortable life as a prince to become an aesthetic to meditate on the causes of pain in this life, he did not go to an organization to bargain for anything spiritual. True, the Buddha formed the Buddhist religion, but he made it clear to participants of Buddhism that they had to rely upon their own efforts; all Buddhism provided was a series of practices one should follow in this effort. This is evident from the Buddha's comment on his deathbed, "Be diligent in your efforts to gain liberation[137]." This comment makes it clear — one's liberation, enlightenment, or salvation is purely a product of one's diligence; it is not something that one can purchase from a religious institution.

THE PROBLEMS WITH MATERIALISTIC THEORIES ABOUT THE ORIGIN OF RELIGION

All of the theories discussed above are pseudoscientific, because, although they may involve elaborate "scientific" reasoning, none of them can be falsified. As pointed out in chapter four, a theory can be considered scientific only if it can be falsified. None of the theories presented above can be scientifically tested, consequently, none of them are truly scientific. They all suffer from one critical problem – they insist on studying the objective aspects of religion without touching the subjective experience. I have noted from the beginning of the book that the religious experience is real, although obviously very subjective. Hence, studying religion from a scientific (i.e. objective) starting point entirely misses the internal experience that makes religions so vibrant and vital. In a way, a materialist making a "scientific" study of religion is akin to an art critic praising a painting by saying that the paint is composed of the finest natural pigments and is painted on the most expensive parchment available, without ever mentioning the image that is in the painting.

To understand how the "scientific" study of religion is inherently flawed, consider what scientists from an alien planet would think if they analyzed human culture. They might come up with a theory to explain religion that is very similar to one of those listed above. Wouldn't the evolution of science also be a mystery to them? They obviously would have observed that modern industrial society had evolved alongside modern science. This would probably lead to a functionalist view of science. The aliens might theorize that physics evolved to provide the machines necessary for modern life, chemistry evolved to produce the many complex chemicals a modern society needs, and geology evolved to provide the natural resources necessary to produce the machines and to obtain the fuels necessary to run them. The alien theorists, however, would have a tough time understanding the development of "curiosity-driven" science, just as the officials in the Reagan administration did, when they coined that term to disparage research that had no immediate monetary gain. Why would a scientist spend his whole life studying ants, as did the famous atheist E.O Wilson, when all one needs to get rid of them is a little well-applied insecticide? Why would a scientist spend his life studying snails on a desert island, as did the agnostic, but strongly materialistic, Stephen Jay Gould, when there is no obvious benefit to the study?

The scientists who comment on the evolution of religion, such as Richard Dawkins, E.O Wilson, and Stephen Jay Gould, don't have a functionalist view of science, nor do they worry about the origin of "curiosity-driven" science because they are immersed in scientific culture. They know the thrill of discovery that makes "curiosity-driven" science so appealing, and therefore, they never bother to wonder how science evolved. However, the religious experience is completely alien to them. Without understanding the importance of that experience, they are forced into a functionalist view of religion, which leads to wildly improbable explanations for how religion began.

CHAPTER 8

The Practices of the Various Religions

INTRODUCTION

The arguments that atheists use against religion reflect a strong bias they have toward positivism, which is the philosophical concept that only objective knowledge is valid. To atheists the religious experience has no relevance, because, by definition, it is highly subjective. This book has assembled many arguments stressing the reality of the religious experience, but to many atheists these arguments are not compelling because the experience they are describing is subjective, and hence, according to positivism, is not a convincing objective truth. Because the religious experience is a subjective phenomenon, it cannot be proven by any scientific experiment and, therefore, to someone who considers that linear thinking is the only way to understand reality, the religious experience has no validity.

However, there is a strong objective argument one can make about the reality of the spiritual experience, namely that the practices of the world's religions are all highly similar. Although the religions of the East and West are graced with a wide variety of doctrines, they share a very limited number of practices, which, the various religions contend, are designed to lead the practitioner to the religious experience. We can study religious practices in much the same way that a biologist studies how honey bees use their waggle dance to transmit information. When a foraging honey bee returns to the hive it will do a dance with various moves that informs other bees about the distance and direction toward food or water. We cannot know what the bees are thinking when they do this (if they think!), but scientists can still study their dances to understand how they communicate. In a similar way, we can study the practices of religions to understand how the religious experience is transmitted. Just as scientists cannot explain what a bee is thinking when it is dancing, in this book I will not make a great effort to explain why these practices work, given that each religion has its own explanation of them. I will, however, argue that the commonality of religious practices demonstrates, rather conclusively, that the spiritual experience is a human reality.

PRACTICES

PRAYER. To some extent, most religions depend on prayer as a way for a person to contact the divine, although how one defines the "divine" depends on the religion in question. Certainly, for monotheistic religions, the divine manifests primarily as God. In addition to God, there are many other manifestations of the divine to which people pray. Many religions consider the divine to be manifest in humans of great spiritual development. This includes the founders of religions, such as Jesus, Mohammed and the Buddha. It also includes major teachers within most religions. A good example of this practice is Guru yoga, which is devoted to the teachers who helped establish the various schools of Tibetan Buddhism. In a similar practice, Catholics venerate a pantheon of saints who they envision to possess divine power. For some religions, the divine also includes non-temporal beings such as deities and angels; practitioners may pray to them for assistance or guidance.

In addition to the diversity of concepts of the divinity to which it is directed, prayer also manifests a wide variety of practices. Every religion tends to have its own practices, postures, and intentions known as prayer. Huxley recognizes four types of prayer: petition, intercession, adoration, and contemplation[138].

Petition and intercession: In petitionary prayer, one asks the divine for assistance in solving one's problems; in intercessory prayer, one supplicates the divine to assist another person. One could consider these two types of prayer as *supplicational* prayers, in which a person asks for help from an outside divine being. These are the types of prayers that atheists, who are not familiar with the details of religious practices, think of when they encounter the word "prayer". To them, the efficacy of these types of prayers is questionable, no matter how evident it may be to the religious practitioner. For example, if I pray for sunny weather on Sunday because I am planning a picnic and the weather that day is fabulous, who is to say that the weather is nice only because I had prayed for it? Using this argument, atheists contend that people who believe that their prayers are answered are deluded folks who still cling to primitive beliefs about the nature of reality.

The certainty with which atheists dismiss supplicational prayer evaporates when one discusses prayers of adoration and contemplation, which one could classify as *realizational* prayers, because one uses these prayers as practices aimed at attaining psychological changes on how one views and approaches the world.

Adoration: In adoration prayer one visualizes the characteristics of a holy person, be it a saint or a deity, and tries to maintain complete concentration on the visualization. This type of prayer occurs in some types of Christianity, such as in prayer using the icons of the Orthodox Church, and it is particularly common in Hinduism and in Tibetan Buddhism. The ultimate goal of this type of prayer is to dissolve one's ego into the deity that is being visualized. The result of this kind of prayer, which may not occur until after many years of practice, is an experience in which the object being visualized comes to life in one's mind. This experience is similar to Ramakrishna's visualization of Mahakali, black and shiny, arising from a golden ocean, that was described in chapter two of this book.

Contemplative prayer: Contemplative prayer is the highest level of prayer during which one abandons one's interior dialogue and becomes entirely open to the divine presence. Contemplative prayer is a traditional Christian prayer that dates back to the Gospel of Matthew.

> But whenever you pray, go into your room, and shut the door and pray to your Father who is in secret; and your Father who sees in secret will reward you[139].

The Trappist monk Thomas Keating interprets this quote to mean the following:

1. Leaving behind the external turmoil, the environment we may be in, and the concerns of the moment by entering our inner room, the spiritual level of our being, the level where our intuition and spiritual will reside.

2. Closing the door, that is shutting out and turning off the interior conversation we normally have with ourselves all day long as we judge, evaluate, and react to people and events entering and leaving our lives.

3. Praying in secret to the Father, who speaks to us beyond the sound of words[140].

Contemplative prayer was common in monasteries in Medieval times, but it lost popularity during the Reformation:

> With the suppression of monasteries in many European countries during the Reformation, and the Inquisition's persecution of individuals that practiced certain forms of quiet prayer that were deemed suspect by the church, contemplative prayer faded into a rarified practice appropriated for cloistered monks well advanced on the spiritual journey but not for the laity[141].

The practice of contemplative prayer is not easily accessible; the depths of it require extensive practice. There are several ways one can develop ability in ease into contemplative prayer. One process, as outlined by St. Teresa of Avila, first involves verbal prayer, then mental prayer, and finally contemplative prayer.[142] In verbal prayer, a person concentrates on a simple prayer such as the Lord's Prayer, this mode of prayer evolves into mental prayer as the person begins to concentrate on the meaning of the words in the prayer. As a person delves deeply into the meaning of the words, slowly the words fall away and the prayer becomes mental prayer. Over time, in mental prayer, the discursive activity would eventually fade away and one would slip into contemplative prayer.

Thomas Keating, who popularized contemplative prayer in the late 20th century presented another means of attaining contemplative prayer. He advised that, because it is difficult to jump right into contemplative prayer, the best way is to start with centering prayer[143]. The goal of centering prayer is to let go of all our agendas and expectations. We do this by relying on a sacred symbol, such as a word from the Scripture, a sense of God, an image of holiness, or to our breath. Whenever one finds that one has been carried away by thoughts, one uses the sacred symbol as a way to bring one back to centering prayer. By bringing oneself back again and again to the sacred symbol, the tendency to wander into thoughts slowly wanes. As one settles into this interior silence, the sacred symbol is no longer needed and centering prayer grades into contemplative prayer. This process doesn't involve shutting off the interior dialogue, but simply not being attached to thoughts, and just letting them float by.

> As long as we find that we are attracted to thoughts or feelings going by on the level of our memory or imagination, we freely make use of the sacred word not to push thoughts away, but to reaffirm our original intention of consenting to God's presence[144].

Fr. Keating compares our consciousness to a flooded river clogged with floating debris. The debris represents the thoughts and emotions that continually arise in our egos. Normally, we tend to identify ourselves with those thoughts and emotions that continually flow though our minds and are not aware that they must be flowing along on something.

> That something is the inner stream of conscious-ness, which is our participating in God's being[145].

Those who advocate centering or contemplative prayer maintain that it works, because when one ceases to be involved or attached to our discursive mind, or the debris that is flowing along the surface of our consciousness, then we can know that we are more than our thoughts. Instead one becomes aware of a deeper level of consciousness that arises from a divine source.

MEDITATION: Before discussing meditation, it is important to note that the word means different things in different religions.

> In Christianity, the term *meditation* ...traditionally meant the active use of the intellectual facilities to reflect on the nature of God or truth, while the term *contemplation...* meant the non-conceptual experience of "resting in God", or in truth itself (author's italics)[146].

In contrast, in Sufism the words mean quite the opposite:

> Contemplation...refers to the process of deepening reflection, while meditation...refers to awareness without thought content[147].

It's important to note that the Sufi definition for the words "meditation" and "contemplation" are also what Eastern Religions mean when they use those words. To eliminate confusion, in this book, when I use the words *meditation* and *contemplation*, I will try to make it clear by the context whether the words carry the connotation of Christianity or of the Eastern Religions. I will use *contemplative practices* to refer to mindful practices done in any major religion; this will include both meditation and contemplative prayer.

Meditation, as defined by the Buddhists and Hindus, is a major spiritual practice that has very ancient roots. Artifacts showing deities in the meditation position have been found in the Indus valley dating back to ca. 2000 BCE, suggesting that meditation in India dates from well before the formulation of Hinduism or its derivative, Buddhism[148]. The goal of meditation is to watch one's mind. To do this, one sits in a comfortable pose and looks downward with a gentle gaze. In Asia the usual way to sit is in the lotus position, in which legs are crossed with the right foot on the left thigh and the left foot on the right thigh. Once one is settled in a comfortable posture (the lotus position is not needed), one chooses an "anchor". This is an object of meditation, to which one returns whenever one finds that he or she has been lost in thought. The anchor may be a word or an object or a small statue or image. In many traditions the breath is used as the anchor. During meditation, one simply keeps the object of meditation in mind. For most people starting to meditate, it takes just a few seconds before thoughts arise and carry one's attention away. When one finds oneself lost in thought, the instructions are simple — merely come back to the anchor.

For most of us, this is what meditation entails, finding our anchor, getting lost in thought, coming back to the anchor, and quickly getting lost in thought again. On the surface it seems inane to sit in a chair or cross-legged on a cushion and letting yourself get lost in thought time and time again. However, if one keeps the practice up long enough, subtle changes begin to happen. First, by coming back to the anchor again and again, and watching thoughts vanish, some of which may be very vivid, one slowly begins to see those thoughts simply as empty energy. One also begins to recognize emotions as being only thoughts and, with this insight, slowly the emotional turmoil of life, which sometimes seems so powerful, becomes less gripping. Over time, one might also realize that the persona that one presents to others is also simply a construct of one's thoughts — there is nothing behind those thoughts. This helps loosen the grip that one's ego — one's plans, expectations, and opinions — has on one's life.

All of these insights help a person to develop equanimity, to be able to ride out the ups and downs of life. Meditation leads to greater benefits than this:

> If we rest and do nothing at all and just experience whatever arises, the awake quality of the mind is naturally present. Practice consists of recognizing that quality, keeping in touch with it and trusting it[149].

In other words, one recognizes that all those thoughts that have been troubling oneself are riding on an ineffable mind. Consequently, just as in contemplative prayer, when one becomes adept in meditation, one realizes that the thoughts are merely like debris flowing along the surface of the river, and that consciousness is the river itself.

A sizable proportion of Western Buddhists maintain that Buddhism is superior to other religions because it is non-theistic and it provides practices without requiring a person to accept any beliefs[150]. Of course, this lack of dogmatism is what drew me to Buddhism in the first place. However, as I learned more about the mystical traditions in other religions, I slowly realized that this opinion is simply wrong; the mystical traditions of most religions have more in common than is generally recognized. A good example of this commonality is seen in the fact that meditation and contemplative prayer are essentially the same techniques. The differences between them consist only in the symbols involved in each practice or how one describes the indescribable. Those who strongly argue over which religion has the best symbols to express the ineffable are making the error of mistaking the finger that is pointing at the moon for the moon itself.

YOGA: Today yoga is widespread in the West, where most people think of it as a group of poses one has to master to gain some degree of physical fitness. Few people realize that yoga is, in itself, a complete spiritual practice. The practice of yoga, which goes back to the earliest days of civilization in the Indus valley, was formalized by Patañjali in the second century AD in *The Yoga Sutra*. In this manuscript he outlines the eight aspects of yoga:

I. **Yama - Universal morality:** Patañjali notes that once one recognizes that one's individuality is part of the matrix of life, one becomes averse to hurting others, and yama arises spontaneously. This behavior includes the practice of compassion for all living things, commitment to truthfulness, non-stealing, sense control, and lack of desire for material goods.

2. **Niyama - Personal discipline:** These disciplines include cleanliness, contentment, awareness of the present moment, disciplined use of energy, self-examination, and celebration of the spiritual. In other words, surrender to the unknown.

3. **Asanas – Postures:** Asanas are the body postures that one associates with yoga. The postures are designed to strengthen the body, improve balance, and develop an inner fitness that helps one produce strength in the other aspects of yoga.

4. **Pranayama – Movement of energy:** Prana is energy that pervades the body; it is often equated with the breath. Pranayama includes exercises that help control the breath and direct the flow of energy throughout the body. Pranayama also involves control of one's life-force.

5. **Pratyahara – Non-attachment:** This translates to withdrawal from that which nourishes the senses. In practice this is seen as non-attachment to those sensory distractions that distract one from the path of self-realization.

6. **Dharana – concentration:** This term means the immovable concentration of the mind. The mind is stilled to achieve the state of complete absorption.

7. **Dhyana – Devotion:** This means devotion or meditation on the divine. In this state one reaches liberation or moksha.

8. **Samadhi – Meditative absorption:** In the state of samadhi the body and senses are at rest as if asleep, but the mind and reason are awake. One drops the sense of being distinct from the surrounding world and rests in a sense of non-duality.

Many of these aspects of yoga are common to other religions. Yama and niyama, morality and personal discipline; are found in most religions, pratyahara, withdrawal from sensual stimulation, is common to religions that contain monastic disciplines; and dharana, and samadhi are found in other religions that practice meditation or contemplative prayer. Only two features are distinctive of yoga: asanas and pranayama.

Pranayama. Pranayama yoga includes practices that are designed to concentrate the flow of energy (prana) through our body. The teachings of pranayama yoga contend that, in addition to our physical body, we also have a subtle, or mystical, body that consists of centers of yogic energy that are arrayed along our spine. These centers are called *chakras,* which is Sanskrit for "wheel". Yogic teachings recognize four to seven chakras that are spread from the base of the spine to the top of the head. These chakras are located: 1) at the base of the spine, 2) at the level of the sex organs, 3) the solar plexus, 4) the heart, 5) the throat, 6) between the eyebrows, and 7) at the top of the head. The exact number chakras in a yogic practice is dependent on the teachings of that particular practice. Some teachings combine chakras one and two and some ignore one or more of the other chakras. As one moves from the lower chakras to the upper chakras one moves from baser to more spiritual values. For example, the first chakra is related to basic existence and the second is related to sexual energy, whereas the seventh chakra is related to pure consciousness.

The goal of pranayama is to open the chakras by visualizing moving energy in a process called *kundalini* from the base of your spine upward through each chakra. As one opens each chakra one progressively refines one's spiritual qualities. Opening the first chakra helps connect one with the Earth, opening the second chakra enhances one's creative abilities, and opening the third chakra helps fulfill one's intentions. Opening the heart chakra improves one's connections with all beings in one's life, and opening the throat chakra improves one's ability to communicate with others. Finally, opening the sixth chakra helps one to recognize one's purpose in life, and opening the seventh chakra helps one to recognize one's unlimited and unbounded nature[151].

Asanas. The poses, or the asanas, are the aspect of yoga that most people are acquainted with. Regular practices with the poses bring awareness into one's body and build balance, agility, and strength. The poses also have a role in distributing prana, and in classical yoga asanas are integrated with pranayama. As yoga has become widespread in the West, it has become a physical practice that is focused on the asanas. This concentration on the physical, rather than the spiritual aspects, however, doesn't mean that the yoga practiced in the West doesn't carry a spiritual aspect. For example, when one "breathes into" difficult spots while holding a particular asana, one is practicing a type of awareness because, in the process, one is focusing attention on how the mind interacts with the body. When the mind relaxes as one lets go of a difficult pose, it helps one become aware of the depth of quietude that exists within the mind behind all of our thoughts.

Yoga is primarily a Hindu practice, however, both Buddhism and Jainism, which are derived from Hinduism, use yogic practices. Yoga, particularly pranayama, provides important practices in Tibetan Buddhism. During the past fifty years yoga has not only assumed an important secular role in Western culture, it has also become a subsidiary practice in many contemplative practices, including in some Christian and Jewish groups (see chapter nine).

SCRIPTURE AND RITUAL: One can do the practices listed above, prayer, meditation, and yoga alone, although there are certainly environments where they are done as part of group practice. An important feature about religions is that they produce communities and community practices involve scripture and ritual. Nearly all religions have a written scripture, writings that are designed to help the reader understand the nature of the divine, at least as that particular religion envisions it. In her book *The Lost Art of Scripture. Rescuing the Sacred Texts*, Karen Armstrong maintains that scripture and ritual grew up together. Traditionally, scripture was not read so much as sung or chanted so that the words of the scripture along with the symbols and physical actions of the ritual interacted with the intuitive nature the listener's mind, allowing one to see through one's own ego so one can understand the nature of Ultimate Reality.

> First, we have seen that scripture was always heard in the context of ritual, which dramatized it and enabled the participants to embody it. Music, a product of the right hemisphere of the brain, stilled the analytical thinking of the left side of the brain and gave participants intimations of a more mysterious dimension of reality that transcended their mundane experience. It evoked attitudes of wonder, respect and reverence for the cosmos and other human beings[152].

In addition to the importance of scripture to the community established around religions, intense study of scriptures by mystics, independent from ritual, has become an important path to spiritual insight. A very good example of this mystical way to study scripture is *Lectio Divina* (divine reading), which is a way of studying the Bible that has been part of monastic practice in the Catholic Church since the Middle Ages. Mystics maintain that there are multiple levels of understanding scripture:

The monks of the Middle Ages called these different levels the "four senses of Scripture." The senses of Scripture are not four ways of discussing a particular text on a rational level. They are four levels of listening to the same passage. The teaching presupposes that Scripture contains a mysterious dynamic that moves one to ever deeper levels of understanding the word of God. These are the literal, the moral, the allegorical, and the unitive...

...The first, or literal sense of Scripture is the historical message and example of Jesus. But when we engage the gospel through Lectio Divina, we begin to put what it says into practice...When we begin to put into practice and live by the Scripture, we have reached the moral stage...

...As we read the gospel and interiorize the events in which Jesus brings his disciples and friends, we ourselves move beyond the moral sense into the allegorical sense of Scripture. It slowly dawns on us that the gospel is about *us*; that our own life is mirrored in its pages...

The fourth level of Scripture is the unitive...That takes place when you are so immersed in the word of God that the word is coming out of you as a kind of continuing revelation[153].

The Jewish mystical tradition, the Kabbalah uses a similar intense study to extract the mystical truths of the Torah. Kabbalists recognize

> ...four senses of scripture: *peshat*, the literal sense, *remez*, allegory, *derash*, the moral sense, and *sod*, their own mystical interpretation of the Torah... Scripture was crucial to the Kabbalah. Whenever he studied the scripture the Kabbalist descended into the text and into himself — a descent that was also an ascent into the source of being. God and scripture were inseparable, because scripture embodied the divine in human language ...[154]

In a similar way that Catholic monks studied the Bible and Kabbalists studied the Torah, the Sufis also note that the Quran also lends itself to several levels of interpretation, as noted by Rumi:

> There is an outer form to the Qur`an
> Its inner is more powerful though, good man,
> And inside that there's even a third layer —
> All intellects would lose themselves in there.
> The fourth layer inside none have seen at all
> But God, Who's peerless and incomparable[155].

Intense study of the scriptures of Abrahamic religions is designed to lead to a deeper understanding of reality. A similar sense exists in Buddhism, where study of scripture is said to involve "listening, contemplation, and meditation." The student first listens closely to the guru's teaching. In these days when so much of the Buddhist teachings have been written down, the word "listening" could be replaced by "reading". After one has heard, or read, a teaching, one actively cogitates on it, contemplating on how the words fit together. Finally, maybe days or weeks later, during one's daily meditation practice, an insight into the meaning of the teachings may arise. When this happens, one can claim the teachings as one's own.

SURRENDER AND SELF-EFFACEMENT. A common feature about the practices described above is that they tend to lessen the ego's hold on one's mind. In this context, the ego is the stream of chatter, judgements, and opinions that constantly fill our minds. It is said that God speaks in whispers and that, for most of us, these whispers are drowned out by the raucous chatter in our minds. World's religions agree that one cannot break through to understand the spiritual nature of the world without dropping the continual mental gossip that is generated by one's ego. As Huxley says:

> Every enhancement of the separate personal self produces a corresponding diminution of that self's awareness of divine reality...[156]

This process of dropping one's fixation on oneself goes by different names in different religions. For example, the very name of the Muslim religion, *Islam,* which means "surrender", is a direct reminder that one has to drop one's sense of "me" to attain religious insight. The name implies that a person cannot access the heart of the Islamic religion without dropping one's concepts, interests, and goals, and surrendering to the will of Allah. In Islam, as in most religions, one is encouraged to die to the normal self:

> When they say "Die before ye die," they do not mean to assert that the lower self can be essentially destroyed, but that it can be purged of its attributes, which are wholly evil. These attributes — ignorance, pride, envy, uncharitableness, etc. — are extinguished, and replaced by the opposite qualities, when the will is surrendered to God and the mind is concentrated on Him[157].

A term describing the same process that is commonly found in the Christian religion is "self-mortification". This doesn't mean flagellating oneself with sticks or whips, as the name would imply. Instead, as St. Teresa of Avila says:

> This internal mortification is acquired, as I have said, by proceeding gradually, not giving into our own will and appetites, even in little things until the body is completely surrendered to the spirit[158].

When one is quietly sitting in contemplative prayer or in meditation, letting the thoughts in one's mind drift by like clouds in the sky, when one is using one's whole attention visualizing a deity, like Jesus, or when one is deeply concentrating on relaxing muscles in a difficult yoga pose, the chatter of the mind is quieted and one is closer to experiencing the divine. Unfortunately, just by easing into an egoless state, one doesn't automatically slide into a spiritual experience. It usually takes a significant time in prayer or meditation to obtain religious insight.

THE PROTEAN NATURE OF RELIGIOUS PRACTICE

A distinctive feature about the spiritual practices described above is that most of them appear across various religions, even religions that have highly different doctrines. There are two possible explanations for this commonality. One explanation is that the common practices were exchanged between two religions as they came in contact. The other is that practices were developed independently in various religions. A good example of practices that were derived from contact between religions is the practice of yoga, which occurs in Hinduism and its derivative religions Buddhism, especially Tibetan Buddhism, and Jainism. It is likely that as these religions broke off from, or interacted with, Hinduism they adopted yoga and applied it to their own doctrines. Good examples of practices that appear to have developed independently in different religions include meditation and various types of prayer as well as intense contemplation of scriptures. These practices are widespread in religions that probably were not in contact until the 20th century.

A good example of how different practices have arisen in a single religion is the historical development of Buddhism. Although religious practices vary within all religions, the changes in Buddhism are particularly striking. In his original teaching in the fifth century BCE, the Buddha formulated a religion where the practices were based entirely on meditation. Prayer, particularly supplicational prayer, was not part of the practices. In addition, the Buddha strongly discouraged any metaphysical speculation, as indicated by this quote:

> The Buddha always told his disciples not to waste their time and energy in metaphysical speculation. Whenever he was asked a metaphysical question, he remained silent. Instead, he directed his disciples toward practical efforts. Questioned one day about the problem of the infinity of the world, the Buddha said, "Whether the world is finite or infinite, limited or unlimited, the problem of your liberation remains the same." Another time he said, "Suppose a man is struck by a poisoned arrow and the doctor wishes to take out the arrow immediately. Suppose the man does not want the arrow removed until he knows who shot it, his age, his parents, and why he shot it. What would happen? If he were to wait until all these questions have been answered, the man might die first." Life is so short. It must not be spent in endless metaphysical speculation that does not bring us any closer to the truth[159].

It is clear that the Buddha's view was that the religion he had developed was designed primarily to alleviate suffering of humans, it was devoid of any metaphysical speculation and certainly devoid of petitionary practices. The root of Buddhism is the four noble truths: 1) life is suffering, 2) suffering is caused by wanting reality to be other than it is, 3) you can make suffering cease, and 4) meditation is the key to removing suffering. As the Buddha said to his disciples as he lay dying, "Be a light unto yourselves", which means that each person has the resources necessary to attain realization. This type of Buddhism, which is strongly based on meditation and is devoid of metaphysical speculation, still survives as Theravada and Zen Buddhism, the Buddhism practiced in South Asia and Japan.

Tantric Buddhism, or Vajrayana Buddhism arose in India by the seventh century of the common era and within a few hundred years was transmitted to Tibet. Tantric Buddhism was destroyed in India by the invasion of the Muslims, but it survived in Tibet until the Chinese holocaust of 1959, which spread its seed around the world. Tibetan Buddhism differs significantly from Theravada or Zen Buddhism because, in addition to meditation, it employs many other techniques, such as yoga. to attain realization. In addition it is strongly devotional. It contains practices such as guru yoga, which supplicates the major teachers in each lineage, and deity yoga, a meditation technique that visualizes various meditational deities. These practices were clearly borrowed from Hinduism because the deities of Vajrayana Buddhism are essentially the same as the Hindu deities. The big difference is that in Vajrayana Buddhism, the deities are considered to be part of one's mind, not external forces as in Hinduism.

About the same time that Vajrayana Buddhism was developing in India, another type of Buddhism, called "Pure Land" Buddhism, began to develop. Pure Land Buddhism is based upon the belief that it is too difficult to become enlightened in this corrupt world. Practitioners of this brand of Buddhism therefore endeavor to be reborn in Sukhavati, the "pure land" where one could easily attain enlightenment. To make this happen, they supplicate Amitabha Buddha, the Buddha of this Pure Land, for rebirth in Sukhavati. Pure Land Buddhism spread to China, Japan, and Tibet, where its practices were incorporated into Tibetan Buddhism. It has become the major school of Buddhism in Japan. Although Pure Land Buddhism adheres to the major teachings of Buddhism, such as the four noble truths, its practices totally rely on supplicational prayer. In this way, the practices of Pure Land Buddhism are clearly different from the meditation practiced in Theravada or Zen Buddhism. The prayers of Pure Land Buddhism look superficially like supplicational prayers in Christianity, but Pure Land Buddhism arrived in Japan around the 10th century and was well established by the time the first Christian missionaries arrived in the 16th century, thus, it is evident that the supplicational practices of Pure Land Buddhism evolved independently of similar practices in Christianity.

Along with changes in practices of the various sects of Buddhism over time, the metaphysics of the religion has also changed dramatically. Unlike the total lack of metaphysics in the original religion, both Tibetan Buddhism and Pure Land Buddhism have a rich metaphysical basis. Obviously, if one did not believe that the spiritual realm of Sukhavati existed, where one can be reborn after death, and that is presided over by the red Amitabha Buddha, then one would not consider participating in the practices of Pure Land Buddhism.

WHAT THE COMMONALITY OF RELIGIOUS PRACTICES TELL US

From the discussion above, it is evident that the similarity of practices across many religions can be explained in two ways. Either similar practices evolved independently within various religions or the practices were exchanged between religions. The ways that similar practices have appeared within various religions strongly resemble aspects of evolution known as *parallel evolution* and *reticulate evolution*. This comparison does not imply that the practices arose by Darwinistic processes, but that the development of religious practices responded to external forces in a way that is similar to the development of parallel evolution and reticulate evolution in nature.

Parallel evolution is a process whereby different species evolving in the same environment develop similar shapes. For example, animals evolving in water tend to develop streamlined bodies. As a result, an ichthyosaur, an extinct reptile, and a porpoise, a mammal, have a body that looks like that of a fish. The ichthyosaurs and porpoises evolved from four-legged animals that had originally lived on land and later adopted a marine way of life. As they evolved, ichthyosaurs and porpoises developed their streamlined shape because that shape provided the most efficient way of moving through water. Because a streamlined shape gives an animal living in water an evolutionary advantage, animals living in water evolve to become streamlined.

Reticulate evolution involves a wholesale exchange of genes that takes place between single-celled creatures. If the genes provided in this exchange produce valuable changes in the offspring, then a new genetic lineage will develop. Clearly, if the exchange did not introduce valuable genes to the offspring, reticulate evolution would not have taken place.

One can argue that, in a way similar to how parallel evolution reflects evolution's response to external forces, similar religious practices have developed independently because those practices have precisely the properties that are most effective for accessing a spiritual experience. Likewise, the exchange of practices between various religions takes place because those practices work. If the practices did not have an effect, they would have been dropped, just as genes exchanged between single-celled animals that are not beneficial disappear from the gene pool. Thus, the fact that religions throughout history have developed similar practices or have exchanged those practices between each other provides objective evidence that religious practices work. In other words, as the world's religions contend, the spiritual dimension exists and the practices inherent in various religions help open people to that dimension.

According to these arguments, the exchange of practices between religions or the appearance of similar practices in religions with widely different doctrines can only be explained if these practices were accessing the spiritual experience. It is not logical to assume that they would have been retained, even though they didn't work, simply because long ago someone advised a group of people to do them. The arguments of atheists, who dismiss religious practices as simply empty rituals, cannot explain why similar practices appear in very different religions. Clearly if rituals were empty of spiritual meaning, why would similar practices have appeared in religions with very different doctrines?

CHAPTER 9

Dawn at Last

Over the past few centuries the industrial revolution has completely transformed our world. Today we have an economy, a transportation system, communication abilities, and a medical system that would have seemed magical even a century ago. This amazing transformation hasn't come without a cost. As our economy has grown, materialism has become the dominant worldview, almost as if by concentrating on the physical world of relative reality we drew a black drape around us, separating us from the brilliance of Ultimate Reality that lies beyond it. The main goals of society have become to produce ever more material goods. The intangible values of human life, the importance of the natural environment, and spirituality seemed to have been left outside of the dark cloak of materialism. Early on, for example, in the 19th century, the concentration on materialism without attention to those intangible values had only limited impact on our quality of life, because there were huge expanses of open land beyond human habitation that afforded abundant space for humans to expand into and contained ample resources to be exploited. Indeed, the unprecedented economic growth in the first half of the twentieth century, despite the two horrific world wars, made it look as if this amazing growth could go on forever.

Today our society is showing signs of deep structural problems that are directly tied to the materialism upon which it is built. The intangible values that could easily be ignored a century or more ago are becoming increasingly urgent to address. Because it has ignored those values in the past, our materialistic society has become inherently inequitable and unjust, blind to environmental damage, and emotionally unfulfilling. Our society is inequitable and unjust because in materialism, a person's value is determined by the quantity of material resources that he or she owns. In such a society, some people have the luck to be successful, whereas others do not. According to materialists, for those who are not successful, it is simply their misfortune; there is no need for society to do anything about it. Materialism is damaging to the environment because the most important goal for the economy in a materialistic society is expanding the production and consumption of commercial goods. Any environmental side-effects caused by resource extraction, industrial production, or disposal of waste are unimportant. Finally, it is unfulfilling because, in materialism, the only way to gain fulfillment in life is through the accumulation of goods. For some people this goal is enough, but for many others it is deeply unsatisfying.

As a result of being dominated by materialism for more than two hundred years, we have growing disparity in wealth between the richest and poorest people both in the United States and on the Earth as a whole. For example, the United States prides itself on being the richest country on earth but the top 1% of the population has 40 times the income of the bottom 90%.[160] Although Americans tend to applaud our ability to have "the pursuit of happiness", such a pursuit is not available for those on the lower portion of the income ladder. This explains why, in 2018, the Centers for Disease Control and Prevention (CDC) reported that life expectancy for Americans decreased for the third year in a row[161]. The decrease was caused by increases in drug overdoses, liver disease, and suicide, maladies that have been given the term *disorders of despair*. These disorders and the despair that produces them are directly related to the lower quality of life in which many people find themselves stranded. Because materialism lacks a spiritual dimension, we are faced with impending environmental disasters that our government seems unable to deal with. As pointed out by Pope Francis, the environmental problems are, above all, spiritual problems that cannot be solved using the common paradigms of materialism[162].

The only way our society can solve the many problems that beset it is to develop sensitivity to the environmental problems and the inequalities that our economy produces. These are, of course, values that are not part of materialism but are, instead, more closely related to spiritual principles. As Einstein said, "We cannot solve our problems with the same thinking we used when we made them". If our society develops a more spiritual view of the world, that may trigger the change in mindset needed that is required for us to solve our, apparently intractable, social and environmental problems. The key question is how can this change in worldview happen?

Fortunately, after more than two hundred years enshrouded in the darkness of materialism, as we enter the third decade of the 21st century there is evidence that the first glimmers of dawn are appearing. It is interesting that materialism has held on for so long because, as the discussion presented in this book makes evident, the arguments offered by materialists against the existence of spiritual dimensions are shaky at best. As discussed in chapter six, the reasons put forth by materialists to dismiss the presence of a spiritual dimension are not terribly convincing. The root of their problem, as noted before, is that they are trying to disprove, using rational, linear thinking, the veracity of experiences that are intuitive and beyond reason. With such a flimsy rationale, how is it that materialism still maintains such a strong hold on the worldview of our society?

It is easy to understand why materialism became the dominant worldview at the beginning of the scientific revolution. When one is enamored by the elegance and rigor of a rational explanation for physical phenomena, it seems logical to dismiss those aspects of reality that science cannot study as being insignificant or even nonexistent. It is also understandable why materialism was maintained as the major worldview for Western society throughout the 19th century and into the 20th century, because, during that time, the huge changes in Western society driven by science seemed to support the veracity of materialism.

Materialism has remained as the major worldview of the West throughout the 20th century and into the early 21st century, even as science has become less deterministic. This was partially a response to the fact that, at that time, religion was becoming increasingly fundamentalist, relying on unquestioning belief of a literal interpretation of the scriptures, rather than using the scriptures as a tool to lead one toward realization. When religions are presented as simply belief in words written down thousands of years ago in a pre-scientific world, it is easy for materialists to reject them.

Over the past fifty years significant changes have occurred, which, taken together, indicate that Western society is beginning to rediscover the spiritual dimension of the world around us and that at last, the materialistic view of reality appears to be losing its grip on society. Four important trends indicate that significant changes are in process. First, as detailed in chapter four, the deterministic, objective world of reality presented by materialists no longer fits the nature of modern science. Second, religious thinkers have come to realize that developing a non-dualistic way of seeing reality is key to understanding the spiritual dimension. Third, a contemplative, mystical movement has become vibrant in all of the world's religions. Finally, over the past twenty years, contemplative disciplines, which were initially practiced only in the domain of religion, have become common tools to solve problems in contemporary secular society.

MATERIALISM CONTAINS THE ROOTS
OF ITS OWN DEMISE

As I have noted throughout this book, the framework of the materialist worldview is the rational, linear-thinking world of science. The trouble for materialists is that the kind of science they avow, the solid, objective, deterministic science of Newton, was eclipsed by quantum physics more than a century ago. Chapter three described how quantum physics has shown that all matter is basically energy. This means that the solidity of the physical world is *maya* or illusionary, just as the Hindu mystics say. Physics has also described how, at the quantum scale, electrons, the basis of matter, can manifest either as particles or as waves. Whether we see an electron as a wave or a particle depends on the type of experiments we do. Consequently, at least at the quantum scale, there cannot be a purely deterministic, objective view of reality; some degree of subjectivity must be involved.

Materialists might argue that, because quantum mechanics deals with aspects of reality that exist at extremely small scales, it has limited relevance to the "real" macroscopic world that we exist in. However, in recent years the deterministic view of biology, as encompassed by the 'selfish gene theory', has been shattered by epigenetics, the realization that genes can be 'turned on' or 'turned off' by environmental conditions. This indicates that, even in the megascopic world of biology, science cannot be considered deterministic.

Even though it takes considerable time for intellectual advances in science to filter down to the common culture, it is only a matter of time before our culture incorporates into its worldview the realizations of quantum physics and the advances in biology. When that happens, materialism will lose its role as the dominant worldview of reality. After all, it is hard to maintain a materialistic view of the world when the culture realizes that the material world is simply a manifestation of energy.

THE RECOGNITION THAT A HOLISTIC VIEW OF REALITY IS KEY TO UNDERSTANDING SPIRITUALITY

The assumption inherent in the atheistic, materialistic view of religion is that religion is based upon belief in the stories told in the holy scriptures. Using this premise, atheists argue that because the literal interpretation of sacred texts make no sense, there is no God, They also consider that, because the scriptures of all religions disagree on the details of their spiritual life; at most, only one of these doctrines can be correct. Over the past fifty years, a much different way has been presented to describe religion and the religious experience. Rather than being a belief, religion is now considered by many as being derived from an experience. This insight is gained through contemplative practices, which allow one to attain a nondual view of reality. This nondual view has been called holistic or trans-rational thinking. This transition from considering religion to be a matter of belief to recognizing that it is a function of experience has produced a big problem for atheism that atheists cannot simply dismiss. It is easy to argue that someone's belief is wrong by presenting some simple premises and showing, through the application of logic, that conclusions inherent in such a belief are not reasonable. However, it is very difficult to use this kind of reasoning to argue that a person's experience is not valid, because all experiences are intuitive and complex and lie beyond the realm of simple logic. This is particularly true when dealing with the spiritual experience, because so much of a spiritual experience is ineffable. Furthermore, it is becoming increasingly clear from inter-religious conferences, that the experiences gleaned from contemplative practices are similar for most religions. With this view, the argument that religion makes no sense because each religion has a different explanation for the religious experience has become invalid.

It is increasingly clear that the metanoia associated with spiritual practice is built upon a change in worldview from linear thinking (or rational consciousness) to holistic thinking (or trans-rational consciousness)[163]. The recognition that spiritual experience manifests in a trans-rational, or non-dualistic manner[164] and the realization that people must use holistic or non-dualistic thinking to understand the nature of the spiritual world[165], is a major intellectual step in Western society. These concepts represent a critical change in thinking and they provide a direct way to refute the linear thinking of materialism. Although, nearly a century ago, William James' book *The Varieties of the Religious Experience*, emphasized that the religious experience is real, atheists have insisted that this experience is simply some sort of anomalous, transitory function of the brain. Trapped within the world of linear thinking, materialists are caught trying to argue against religion using pre-rational thinking, while being completely unaware that the trans-rational view of religion is entirely different. Atheists, thus, are unable to understand that the window into spirituality involves a way of viewing reality that is different from linear thinking. The recognition that spiritual understanding involves a non-dualistic way of thinking is a challenge to the materialistic way of seeing reality, because materialists are simply not capable of refuting the validity of non-dualist thinking using only linear reasoning. In their world of rational thinking, they consider that understanding a feature is directly related to a belief in various postulates relating to that feature. The concept that, through spiritual practice, people can develop a nondual view of reality and, in the process, can gain intuitive insight into a trans-rational reality, is an idea that is incomprehensible to materialists. As contemplative practices take hold in our society, the concept that holistic (or trans-rational) thinking is required to understand the spiritual dimension will become more widespread, with the result that the materialist view of reality will look increasingly out-of-date.

The Rediscovery of Contemplative Religion

Quietly, almost imperceptibly, over the past fifty years, an amazing transformation has begun taking place in the world's religions. This has involved two closely related phenomena: the introduction of Eastern religions to the West and the re-emphasis of contemplative practices in the Abrahamic religions.

INTRODUCTION OF EASTERN RELIGIONS TO THE WEST.
Tendrils of Eastern religion were penetrating American society as early as the mid-nineteenth century. An English translation of the *Bhagavad Gita* appeared in New England in 1843[166] and was quickly adopted by the American intelligentsia. It was read by Ralph Waldo Emerson, whose essays are commonly filled with comments that could be derived directly from the Hindu texts. As noted by Joseph Goldberg (parentheses are mine):

> In place of a fallen sinful humanity, separate and apart from God, he (Emerson) upheld an ecstatic vision of a divine essence—the "cause behind every stump and clod" as he wrote elsewhere—in which we swim and which swims through us[167].

In his essays and in his lectures presented around Boston, Emerson presented his interpretation of human spirituality that could have come straight from the Vedas.

Henry David Thoreau, like Emerson, considered that the Hindu texts helped illuminate his own spiritual experiences. As he said in *Walden:*

> Whenever I have read any part of the Vedas, I have found that some unearthly and unknown light illuminated me. In the great teaching of the Vedas, there is no touch of sectarianism. It is of all ages, climes, and nationalities, and is the royal road for the attainment of the Great Knowledge.

The Eastern thought avowed by Emerson and Thoreau became the heart of the Transcendental Movement. The Transcendental Club formed in 1836. Although it thrived in New England for only about 20 years, its imprint is still strongly felt today.

> Every American who checks the spiritu-al-but-not-religious box or shuffles off to a medi-tation retreat is squarely in the Transcendentalist lineage[168].

Buddhism was a little tardier in getting a foot-hold in the West than was Hinduism, partly because Buddhism had vanished from India centuries before the British arrived and, therefore, the sacred writings were less accessible to the British colonial-ists. Emerson and Thoreau both mentioned the Buddha in their writings, and Thoreau is credited with helping to translate portions of the *Lotus Sutra* from French, which was published in the Transcendental publication, *The Dial*, in 1844[169]. The major introduction for Westerners to Buddhism, though, didn't come until 1879 with the publication of Sir Edwin Arnold's poem *The Light of Asia or The Great Renunciation, Being the Life and Teachings of Gautama, Prince of India and the Founder of Buddhism.* The book appeared with rave reviews in America and was immensely popular.

Madame Helena Petrovna Blavatsky, a Russian widow, arrived in New York in 1873 and immediately gained a following. Madame Blavatsky claimed to have been initiated into the higher teachings of Buddhism during her travels in Asia and to have received knowledge telepathically from Oriental spiritual masters. Shortly after arriving in the United States she met Colonel Henry Steel Olcott and in 1875 the two of them were instrumental in founding the Theosophical Society. The Theosophical Society, which still exists today, was founded:

> ...to encourage open-minded inquiry into world religions, philosophy, science and the arts in order to understand the wisdom of the ages, respect the unity of all life, and help people explore spiritual self-transformation[170].

In addition to Buddhism, Madame Blavatsky's view of Theosophy involved a whole range of occult teachings such as the Kabala, Rosicrucianism, and Hermeticism. Even so, the Theosophical Society played an important role in introducing Eastern religions to the West.

Despite the popularity of Eastern religions among American intellectuals during the nineteenth century, it is unlikely that many Americans at that time ever encountered an established teacher in the Buddhist or Hindu religions. All that changed during the World Parliament of Religions that was held in Chicago in 1893 as part of the Chicago Columbian Exposition. The Columbian Exposition ran all summer long; the Parliament of Religions was held during two weeks in September.

The speaker who introduced Hinduism to the World Parliament of Religions was Swami Vivekananda (1863 - 1902), who presented a dynamic talk. He was considered one of the most inspiring speakers at the Parliament.[171] He had toured New

England before the Parliament and for two years afterward he continued his speaking throughout the United States. He helped found the Vedanta Society in New York in 1894. Today the Vedanta Society has more than 20 centers across the United States and Canada.

Several speakers presented talks on Buddhism, including Anagarika Dharmapala from Sri Lanka (then known as Ceylon). Dharmapala, who was 29 at the time of the Parliament, was a dramatic speaker and made quite an impression. During his career which lasted until 1933, he was a tireless missionary for Buddhism, speaking and organizing in the United States, India, and Europe.

Another key speaker about Buddhism was Soyen Shaku, a Zen Abbot. He was not as dramatic a speaker as Dharmapala or Vivekananda because he did not speak English; his translated talk had to be read by a moderator at the Parliament. However, he played a key role in the establishment of Buddhism in America because he sent his student Diasetz Tietaro Suzuki (often referred to as D.T. Suzuki) (1870—1966) to America to teach. D.T. Suzuki had a long teaching career, both in Japan and in the United States. His many books on Buddhism, and particularly on Zen, had immense influence on the growth of Buddhism in the United States.

Throughout the early part of the Twentieth Century, Hinduism and Buddhism slowly established frameworks in the United States, thanks to the influence of such teachers as D. T. Suzuki and Paramahansa Yogananda (1893 -1952), whose 1946 book,

Autobiography of a Yogi, was an instant success. Even so, Eastern religions did not become an important part of American culture until the 50s and 60s. In the mid 1950s, the Beat poets, such as Alan Ginsberg, Gary Snyder, and Jack Kerouac, wrote poems and books that made Zen a common term within American culture. Although the Zen Buddhism of the Beat poets was an eclectic practice at best, their poetry made Americans familiar with Zen and the major tenets of Buddhism.

A similar phenomenon happened in the 1960s with Hinduism. Swami Vishnudevanada came to the United States in 1958, and his book, *The Complete Illustrated Book of Yoga,* the first major illustrated guide to yoga, appeared in 1960. In 1961, Richard Hittleman launched his yoga television show, *Yoga for Health,* which helped him sell millions of copies of his books on yoga. Although the yoga presented by Hittleman strongly emphasized the physical aspects of yoga, the spiritual practices of Hinduism also appeared in the 1960s. Maharishi Mahesh Yogi (1918-2008) developed a distinctive practice he called Transcendental Meditation (TM) in 1955 and held his first world tour in 1958. TM gained fame in the early 1960s when many Hollywood celebrities became attracted to it and it seemed to become main-stream in 1968 when the Beatles visited Maharishi's Ashram in India.

The publicity that the Eastern religions gained in the 1950s and 1960s set the scene for the explosions of meditation and yoga in the 1970s, when a flood of teachers of Eastern religions appeared on the scene. This flood included Asians, such as Suzuki Roshi from Japan, Trungpa Rinpoche from Tibet, Thich

Nhat Han from Vietnam, and Swami Muktananda from India. Along with them were Americans such as Phil Kapleau, Jack Kornfield, Sharon Salzberg, and Ram Dass (whose given name was Richard Alpert). These American teachers had spent years in Asia learning the meditation practices of the Eastern religions, before returning to teach in the United States. Ram Dass' 1971 book *Be Here Now* helped usher in this intense growth in meditation. Throughout the 1970s classes in mindfulness, awareness, and yoga sprang up in cities large and small across the United States and Europe.

The mindfulness and awareness meditation of the Eastern religions fit perfectly into the counter-culture of the 1960s and 1970s, and swiftly attracted thousands of young people. In a society where religion was commonly presented as a set of rules saying "thou shalt" and "thou shalt not", a straight forward spiritual practice that was empirical and not burdened by rules and formalities was a breath of fresh air and thousands embraced it. Meditation and yoga spread widely across the US and Europe throughout the 1960s and 1970s. By the 1980s, there was hardly a city in the West that didn't have a center where people could access teachings on meditation or yoga. In addition, Buddhist retreat centers and Hindu ashrams sprouted up across North America and Europe where students could participate in long-term meditation or yoga retreats. Today, these Eastern practices have become a popular aspect of American culture.

THE RE-ENERGIZING OF MYSTICAL PRACTICES IN THE ABRAHAMIC RELIGIONS. At the same time that the practices of Eastern religions were blossoming in the West, the ancient mystical practices of Christianity and Judaism were being redis-covered and revitalized.

Christianity. The later decades of the twentieth century saw a remarkable growth in contemplative practices in Christianity. This spiritual renewal swept through Christianity in three waves since the 1960s[172]. The first wave arrived in the 1950s and 1960s as writers such as Thomas Merton concentrated on establishing and recording contemplative practice in monastic communi-ties. In the second wave, in the 1970s and 1980s, teachers such as Thomas Keating presented contemplative practices to lay Christians. Today, as the third decade of the twenty-first century opens, we see the third wave in which the senior students of contemplative prayer developed programs and procedures that introduce contemplative practices to the society as a whole.

As noted earlier, contemplation is nothing new to Christianity. It was practiced by the Desert Fathers in the fourth and fifth centuries and was common in Catholic monastic communities in the Middle Ages, as indicated by the writings of St. Teresa of Avila and St. John of the Cross, as well as the anonymous book, *The Cloud of Unknowing.* The combined effects of the Reformation, the Inquisition, and the scientific revolution caused contempla-tion in many of the Christian churches to fade away, although it has been important to the Quakers, who have been honoring silence since the 17th century. Contemplative practices were revi-talized in the early 1970s by three monks from St. Joseph's Abbey in Spencer MA—Fathers William Meninger, Basil Pennington, and Thomas Keating. Thomas Keating had attended a meeting in Rome in 1971 during which Pope Paul VI called upon the visiting monastics to develop a revival of contemplative practice for both monastic and lay people. As a result of this encouragement, Fr. Keating began teaching contemplative prayer at St. Joseph's Abbey. In response to the growing popularity of this practice, in 1983 Fr. Keating lead the first week-long retreat on contemplative prayer. This soon led to the formation of Contemplative Outreach, an organization designed to spread Centering Prayer and Contemplative Prayer throughout the Christian world. Although it had roots in monastic Catholicism, contemplative prayer has become ecumenical. It has not only spread to many denominations of Christianity but also has developed fruitful discussions with other contemplative religions. Since its introduction, contemplative prayer has spread widely within Christian churches, much as Buddhist and Hindu meditation has spread through those who were unaffiliated with Abrahamic religion. In 2018 Contemplative Outreach served over 40,000 people annually and supported over 90 active contemplative chapters in 39 countries[173].

Judaism. The rise of modern contemplative Judaism, which is known as the Jewish Renewal Movement, was spawned by the works of Rabbi Zalman Schachter-Shalomi (1924-2014), who was generally known as Reb Zalman. He was born in Vienna and in 1941 escaped from the Nazis to New York. He became an Orthodox Rabbi in 1947. Inspired by the spiritual awakening of the 1960s and influenced by mystical practices of Christianity, Sufism, and Eastern religions, in 1968 Reb Zalman helped establish the Havurah movement. A *havurah* (or *chavurah,* which is Hebrew for "fellowship") is a small group of Jews that gather to celebrate religious services and who viewed themselves as alternatives to established Jewish institutions. Perhaps the most reasonable date for the beginning of this Jewish Renewal was the publication in 1973 of *The Jewish Catalog: A Do-It-Yourself Kit*[174]. The title of the book was a take-off on the then-popular *Whole Earth Catalog*. It contained the reprint of a book that was self-published in 1958 by Reb Zalman and which may have been the first English book on Jewish meditation. In 1978 Reb Zalman founded B'nai Or ("Sons of Light" in Hebrew), a Jewish Renewal congregation that quickly spread to become a national organization. The organization later changed its name to the gender-neutral P'nai Or ("Faces of Light"). Another landmark in the development of modern Judaism was the publication in 1985 of Rabbi Aryeh Kaplan's book *Jewish Meditation, A Practical Guide*, making practical instructions on ancient Jewish practices available to the general public.

One of the events contributing to the development of contemplative Judaism is the meeting between the Dalai Lama and a group of Rabbis, which included Reb Zelman and Rabbi Jonathan Omer-Man, in 1990[175]. The Dalai Lama wanted advice from the Jewish leaders on how to maintain cultural and spiritual traditions in a population during a diaspora. The rabbis clearly wanted to understand why so many young Jews were abandoning their religion and becoming Buddhists. The conversion of Jews to Buddhism was so prevalent in the 1970s and 1980s that up to 30% of Americans in Buddhist organizations were "JewBus", Buddhists of Jewish origin. When asked about how to keep Jews from abandoning their religion, the Dalai Lama suggested that

Jews should open the doors and open them wide[176]. By this he meant providing students access to the mystical Jewish teachings, many of which were restricted to advanced scholars and were hidden from most mainstream Jews.

Shortly after that meeting with the Dalai Lama in 1993, the national P'nai Or organization joined other organizations to form ALEPH: Alliance for Jewish Renewal, which engendered two principles, Tikkun haLev ("repair of the heart") and Tikkun Olam ("repairing the world") and which became the driving force for the Jewish Renewal. Another force for the Jewish Renewal is the Institute for Jewish Spirituality, which Rabbi Jonathan Omer-Man helped organize in 1998 to infuse Judaism with contemplative practices that originally were thought to be found only in the Eastern religions. Together these two organizations have encompassed the Jewish Renewal Movement, a movement that is designed to revitalize Judaism through the use of a wide variety of spiritual disciplines, including both Jewish spiritual practices from the Kabbalah as well as meditative and yoga practices that have been borrowed from other religious traditions. The Jewish Renewal Movement is an egalitarian organization open to Jews of all religious designations, of both genders and of all sexual orientations.

Islam. The contemplative dimension of Islam, Sufism, has been an aspect of Islam since its very beginning. The Indian philosopher Hazrat Inayat Khan brought Sufism to the United States and Europe in 1910, but the big influx of Sufism came in the 1970s and 1980s[177]. The expansion of Islam into the United States falls into three phases: 1) transplant, 2) hybrid, and 3) perennial[178]. The transplants are mostly foreign-born and their practices are generally traditional to the country of their origin. The hybrids are second generation; they adhere to traditional Islamic practices while trying to accommodate to the culture of Western society. The perennials, in contrast, downplay their Islamic roots while emphasizing the mystical unity of all religions.

The perennial schools of Sufism underwent two significant developments in the 1960s and 1970s. In one, Samuel Lewis, a student of Inayat Khan, introduced a series of interfaith dances that he called the Dances of Universal Peace. The dances, which celebrate the sacred teachings of the world religions, attracted a great following and spread internationally. Today nearly two hundred dance circles meet weekly or monthly in the United States. In the second, Pir Vilayat developed a meditation program that drew heavily on non-Islamic sources such as Buddhism, Yoga, and the mystical teachings of Christianity and Judaism. Vilayat established meditation centers in Europe and the United States[179].

Summary. Many people have argued that the development of contemplative practices in Christianity and Judaism occurred in response to the introduction of meditation by Buddhist and Hindu teachers in the 1960s and 1970s. As noted by Father Thomas Keating:

> "You see a great many Christians had joined one
> or another of the Eastern disciplines over the years
> because they couldn't find any spirituality in the

Christian milieu, whether in churches, parishes or schools, in fact, many had said to me that, had they known that there was a Christian contemplative practice, they wouldn't have gone to the East[180]."

The problem was the same with the Jews who became Buddhists; they saw in Buddhism a spirituality that didn't seem to be present in Judaism. As the poet Alan Ginsberg said:

"What I am getting at—there were no teachers who were clear. Or I didn't run into a teacher who was clear. There may have been some hidden teachers but I didn't know them[181]."

As noted above, however, a close look at the history of religious thought in Christianity and Judaism shows that a rediscovery of contemplative practices was already developing in both religions at the time that Eastern religions invaded the West. This suggests that the introduction of Eastern religions to the West in the 1960s and 1970s did not cause the development of contemplative practices in Judaism and Christianity, but instead helped catalyze the growth of practices that were already under development.

INTERRELIGIOUS DIALOGUE. Religions have interacted frequently throughout history—witness the way, for example, as described in the previous chapter, Tibetan Buddhism incorporated the deities and yoga from Hinduism. However, throughout most of human history, such interaction took place only where empires or civilizations intersected. As long-distance transportation became more efficient in the twentieth century, religious dialogue became more vibrant. Perhaps the first example of this was the Parliament of World's Religions in 1893, which has been previously discussed. When the 1893 Parliament was held, America was mainly a Christian nation that contained small populations of Jews and a smattering of other religions. The presentations on religions other than Christianity produced considerable interest, partially because at the time those religions were so exotic.

The Parliament of World's Religions did not meet again until 1993 (note: it has met five times since then), but there was a huge difference between the 1993 and the 1893 Parliaments. By the time of the second meeting of the Parliament of World's Religions, America, though still dominantly a Christian nation, contained a large population of Jews, Muslims, Hindus, Buddhists, and people of other Eastern religions. Some of the people practicing those religions were descended from the immigrants who had streamed into America in the twentieth century. Others, however, were Americans who had converted to those religions because they felt their new religion spoke to them in a more comprehensive manner than did Christianity or Judaism.

In this melting pot of religions that characterized America, it was not surprising that a healthy communication has developed between various religions. As mentioned in chapter three, one of the major dialogues between religions was the Snowmass Conference, which was held originally at St. Benedict's Monastery in Colorado in 1984 and met in various other places from 1985 until 2004. Wayne Teasdale noted that the depth of the inter-religious dialogue is deeper now than it had been in the past, and defined this period as the *interspiritual age* and noted that a major feature of it is:

> A deep, evolving experience of community between and among the religions through their individual members[182].

This is not to imply that religious dialogue is easy, because it is not. Although religious traditions have similar practices, particularly the contemplative ones, different religions often express the insights gleaned from those disciplines as symbols or metaphors that are mutually contradictory. For example, one has to work hard to see through the surface differences to recognize the commonalities that lie between Christianity and Judaism or Islam and Buddhism. Judging from the comments of Thomas Keating, the organizer of the Snowmass Conferences, this hard work is worth it:

> "Ultimately, I find it liberates one from the aspects of one's tradition that are cultural and are not the essence of the teaching. Usually these have become so intermingled with the essence over the centuries that you cannot discern the difference without being challenged to look at the whole thing from an objective perspective[183]."

A major outcome of these inter-religious dialogues is a sense of convergence among religions, particularly among those that emphasize contemplative practices. By accepting the commonality of the religious experience, while acknowledging that each religion has a unique set of symbols, practices, and rituals to access this experience, these dialogues are evolving toward a common expression of what religion entails, as indicated by the outcome of the Snowmass Conferences, summarized in chapter three. This convergence, of course, is an expression of perennialism, the concept that all religions are trying to access the same ineffable experience. As inter-religious dialogue evolves, it will have a devastating effect on the atheist view of religion, because, religious dialogue will demonstrate that religion is based on experience and not on belief in a simplified, literal interpretation of religious scriptures.

INTRODUCTION OF CONTEMPLATIVE PRACTICE INTO SECULAR LIFE

A key change in American society at the end of the 20th and the beginning of the 21st centuries has been the introduction of contemplative practices to the general public as a way to help reduce the stress and emotional turmoil of life. Key concepts in these practices are to look at thoughts as they come up and to gently dismiss them, a practice that is characteristic of meditation or of centering prayer. When treated in this way, one's thoughts and emotions do not have time to grab one's attention and can be simply released as one returns to meditation or contemplation. Over the past decades, Buddhist, Christian, Hindu, Islamic, and Jewish contemplative communities have presented similar practices to people who are mired in painful and stressful situations[184]. As a result, contemplative practices have been developed as a therapy for a large number of medical and social problems. Some of these difficulties include depression, eating disorders, substance abuse, anger control, chronic pain, attention deficit disorder, grief, diagnosis of a life-threatening illness, or termination of a job[185].

The contemplative practices, which allow people to settle into peace when faced by life's problems, also provide insights into spiritual values, even though the spiritual aspects of these practices are often played down. In a secular environment, the practices are generally presented in a way that is independent of any inherent doctrines. Thus, the secular use of contemplative practices have become a major way that spirituality has been quietly infiltrating society's bastion of materialism. Because they work to decrease tension and enhance a sense of well-being, contemplative practices, such as meditation and yoga, are becoming widespread throughout American society. For example, many more Americans are meditating now than there were just a few years ago. In 2017, 14.2% of the American population had meditated at least once, compared to 4.1% in 2012[186]. Similarly, the practice of yoga has greatly expanded; 20.4 million Americans (8.7% of the population) have practiced yoga, up from 15.8 million in 2004[187]. It is evident that the growing popularity of these practices is happening because people are realizing that they provide a compelling way to address the stresses that arise from living in a secular, demanding, and materialistic society.

Mindfulness practices have also been introduced into the workplace, where they are touted to reduce stress, improve focus, improve creativity, and enhance communication[188]. In short, mindfulness practices can make employees better workers. On the surface, taking a practice designed to lessen a person's ego and using it to enhance a person's ego so that person would fit better into the workplace, seems to be a desecration of a religious practice. However, to me it also shows how mindfulness practice is highly subversive to the materialist mindset. As one realizes that one can use contemplative practices to deal with problems that originally seemed overwhelming, be they medical, social, or related to the workplace, one learns that the mind has amazing powers. This realization becomes a major threat to the materialistic concept that the mind is merely an epiphenomenon of the brain.

CONCLUSIONS

The darkness of materialism, as stifling as it may have been to our society as a whole, did not totally block the light. Throughout the nineteenth and twentieth centuries creative people, starting with Ralph Waldo Emerson and Henry David Thoreau and extending to Thomas Merton and Ram Dass, managed to find paths toward spiritual enlightenment. Those pioneers slowly lifted the dark cloak of materialism that encapsulated the Relative Reality in which we live, showing the brilliant Ultimate Reality that lies beyond. As a result of their efforts, we now live in a society whose materialistic worldview contains large gaps through which the glow of Ultimate Reality shows through. In such an environment, it becomes increasingly possible to realize that physical reality is infiltrated by a spiritual dimension. Thus, it becomes entirely reasonable for one to engage with material-istic linear thinking when dealing with one's every-day life, while at the same time probing the nature of Ultimate Reality using holistic thinking in one's spiritual practice. It is also possible, indeed likely, that in the future, dynamic, creative leaders will open the gaps further and expose our society to the spiritual values we so desperately need to solve the social and environmental problems that overwhelm our society today.

About the Author

Ron Frost is a professor emeritus at the University of Wyoming. For more that forty years he has studied rocks in the mountains of Wyoming and locations elsewhere throughout the world, ranging from Australia to Greenland, trying to decipher the history those rocks record.

For nearly his whole career, he has also studied Tibetan Buddhism. For most of that time he wrestled with the problem of how to reconcile the material world of science with the spiritual world that permeates the world about us. Scientists think that the physical world is as solid as rocks, but mystics consider it as *maya*, an illusion.

To understand why mystics consider the world an illusion, Ron participated in the Three-Year Retreat in Tibetan Buddhism. During the retreat years, 2012-2013, 2014-2015, and 2016-2017, he took temporary ordination as a monk at Gampo Abbey in Nova Scotia and spent up to 11 hours a day in prayer and meditation.

Since coming out of retreat Ron has been active in the Wyoming Interfaith Network, where he is now on the Board of Directors.

Ron as a geologist

Ron as a monk

References

Alumkal, A., 2017, *Paranoid Science, The Christian Right's War on Reality*. New York, New York University Press.

Anonymous, *The Cloud of Unknowing*

Armstrong, K., 2000, *The Battle for God*. New York, Ballantine Books.

Armstrong, K., 2002, *Islam, A Short History*. New York, Random House.

Armstrong, K., 2009, *The Case for God*. New York, Alfred Knopf.

Armstrong, K. 2019, *The Lost Art of Scripture. Rescuing the Sacred Texts*, New York, Alfred A. Knopf.

Arzy, S., and Schurr, R., 2016, "God has sent me to you": Right temporal epilepsy, left prefrontal psychosis. *Epilepsy & Behavior*, 60, 7-10.

Ashbrook, J.B., 1984, Neurotheology: The working brain and the work of theology. *Zygon: The Journal of Religion and Science*, 19, 331- 350.

Azari, N. P., Nickel, J., Wunderlich, G., Niedeggen M., Hefter, H., Tellmann, L., Herzog, H., Stoerig, P., Birnbacher, D., Seitz, R. J., 2001, Neural correlates of religious experience. *European Journal of Neuroscience*, 13, 1649-1652.

Bachelor, S., 1997, *Buddhism Without Beliefs. A Contemporary Guide to Awakening*. New York. Riverhead Press.

Barbour, I.G., 1997, *Religion and Science. Historical and Contemporary Issues*. New York, HarperCollins.

Benítez-Bribiesca, L., 2001, Mimetics: A Dangerous Idea. *Interciencia*, 26, 29-31.

Bergson, H., 1911, *Creative Evolution*. New York, Henry Holt and Company.

Borgman, L., 1998, The Zen of Research, *Journal of Geoscience Education*, 46, 346-353.

Boyd, R and Richardson, P. J., 2000, Meme Theory Oversimplifies How Culture Changes. *Scientific American*, 283, 69 -71.

Brewer, J. A., Worhunsky, P. D., Gray, J. R., Tang, Y.-Y., Weber, J., and Kober, H., 2011, Meditation experience is associated with differences in default mode network activity and connectivity. *Proceedings of the National Academy of Sciences*, 108, 20254-20259.

Bush, M. (ed.), 2011, *Contemplation Nation. How Ancient Practices are Changing The Way we Llive.*, Kalamazoo, MI, Fetzer Institute.

Campbell, J., 1962, *The Masks of God: Oriental Mythology.* New York, The Viking Press.

Chopra, D. and Simon, D., 2004, *The Seven Spiritual Laws of Yoga. A Practical Guide to Healing Body, Mind, and Spirit.* Hoboken, N.J., John Wiley & Sons.

Cullen, M., 2011, Mindfulness-based interventions: An emergent phenomenon. In Bush, M. ed., *Contemplation Nation. How Ancient Practices are Changing the Way we Live.* Kalamazoo, MI, Fetzer Institute. p. 293 – 313.

Cunningham, P. F., 2011, Are religious experiences really localized within the brain? The promise, challenges, and prospects of neurotheology. *Journal of Mind and Behavior*, 32, 223-249.

Davis, D.G., Schmitt, F. A., Wekstein,D.R., and Markesberg, W.R., 1999, Alzheimer neuropathologic alterations in aged cognitively normal subjects. *Journal of Neuropathology and Experimental Neurology*, 38, 376-388.

Dawkins, R., 1976, *The Selfish Gene.* Oxford, Oxford University Press.

Dawkins, R., 2006, *The God Delusion.* New York, Bantam Press.

DeMello, A., 1990, *Awareness: The Perils and Opportunities of Reality.* New York, Image Books.

Dennett, D.C., 1991, *Consciousness Explained.* New York, Little, Brown and Company.

Dennett, D.C., 2006, *Breaking the Spell. Religion as a Natural Phenomenon.* New York, Penguin Books.

Devinsky, O. and Lai, G., 2008, Spirituality and Religion in Epilepsy, *Epilepsy & Behavior*, 12, 636-643.

Dewhurst, K. and Beard, A. W., 1970, Sudden religious conversion in temporal lobe epilepsy. *British Journal of Psychology*, 117, 497-507.

Diamond, J., 1997, *Guns, Germs, and Steel. The fates of human societies.* New York, Norton.

Doyle P., 1997, *Butler's Lives of the Saints,* Collegeville MN. The Liturgical Press.

Ferguson, J. K., 2010, Centering Prayer: A Method of Christian Meditation for Our Time. In. Plante, T. G., ed., *Contemplative Practices in Action.* Santa Barbara, CA, Praeger

Fields, R., 1992, *How the Swans Came to the Lake. A Narrative History of Buddhism in America* 3rd ed.. Boston, Shambhala.

Freemon, F.R., 1976, A differential diagnosis of the inspirational spells of Muhammad the prophet of Islam. *Epilepsia*, 17, 423-427.

Frenette, D, 2011, Christian Centering Prayer in America: A Contemplative Practice for Contemporary America. In Bush, M. ed., *Contemplation Nation. How Ancient Practices are Changing the Way We Live.*, Kalamazoo, MI, Fetzer Institute. p. 75 – 87.

Frost, B. R., 2010, *Religion versus Science. Where both sides go wrong in the Great Evolution Debate.* Washington, D. C., O-Books.

Gabriel, Father, 1965, *The Way of Prayer. A Commentary on Saint Teresa's "Way of Perfection".* San Francisco, Ignatius Press.

Geertz, A. W., 2009, When cognitive scientists become religious, science is in trouble: On neurotheology from a philosophy of science perspective. *Religion*, 39, 319-324.

Goldberg, D. W., 2009, d'Aquili and Newberg's neurotheology: A hermeneutical problem with their neurological solution. *Religion*, 39, 325-330.

Goldberg, P., 2010, *American Veda: From Emerson and the Beatles to Yoga and Meditation How Indian Spirituality Changed the West.* New York, Crown Publishing.

Goleman, D. and Davidson, R. J., 2017, *Altered Traits. Science Reveals How Meditation Changes Your Mind, Brain, and Body.* New York, Avery.

Grandqvist, P., Fredrikson, M., Unge, P., Hagenfeldt, A., Valind, S., Lathammar, D., Larsson, M., 2005, Sensed presence and mystical experiences are predicted by suggestibility, not by the application of transcranial weak complex magnetic fields. *Neuroscience Letters,* 379, 1-6.

Greenberg, A., 2000, *A Chemical History Tour, Picturing Chemistry from Alchemy to Modern Molecular Science.* New York, Wiley Interscience.

Gyurme Dorje (translator), 2006, *Tibetan Book of the Dead.* New York, Penguin Books.

Harris, S., 2004, *The End of Faith. Religion, Terror, and the Future of Reason.* New York, W.W. Norton and Company.

Harris, S., 2014, *Waking Up. A Guide to Spirituality Without Religion,* New York, Simon and Schuster.

Hermansen, M. 1997, In the garden of American Sufism. in Clarke, P., ed. *New Trends and Developments in the World of Islam.* London, Luzac Oriental Press., p. 155-178.

Hitchens, C., 2007, *God is not Great. How Religion Poisons Everything,* New York, Hatchette Book Group.

Hittleman, R, 1983, *Yoga for Health,* New York, Ballantine Books.

Hixon, L., 1992, *Great Swan. Meetings with Ramakrishna.* Boston, Shambhala.

Huxley, A., 1945, *The Perennial Philosophy.* New York, Harper & Brothers.

Inayat-Khan, Z., 2011, Islamic and Islamicate contemplative practices in the United States, in Bush, M. ed., *Contemplation Nation. How Ancient Practices are Changing the Way we Live.,* Kalamazoo, MI, Fetzer Institute, p. 97 - 108.

James, W., 1902, *The Varieties of Religious Experience.* New York, The New American Library.

Kamenetz, R., 1994, *The Jew in The Lotus. A Poet's Rediscovery of Jewish Identity in Buddhist India.* New York, HarperOne.

Kaplan, A., 1985, *Jewish Meditation. A practical Guide.* New York, Schoken Press

Kavanaugh, K. and Rodriguez, O. (translators), 1980, *The Collected works of St. Teresa.* Washington D.C. ICS Publications.

Keating, T., 1986, *Open Mind, Open Heart. The Contemplative Dimension of the Gospel.* London, Bloomsbury Publishing.

Keating, T., 1994, *Intimacy with God. An Introduction to Centering Prayer.* New York, The Crossroad Publishing Company.

Keating, T, 1995, Guidelines for Interreligious Understanding. Points of Agreement and Similarity. In Beversluis, J., *A Source Book for Earth's Community of Religions.* Grand Rapids, MI, CoNexus press. p.148.

Kuhn, T.S., 1962, *The Structure of Scientific Revolutions.* Chicago, University of Chicago Press.

Larson, E. J. and Ruse, M., 2017, *On Faith and Science.* New Haven, Yale University Press.

Lipton, B.H. and Bhaerman, S., 2009, *Spontaneous Evolution.* Carlsbad, Ca. Hay House.

Lonton, A. P., 1979, The relationship between intellectual skills and the computerized axial tomography of children with spina bifida and hydrocephalus. *Zeitschrift für Kinderchururgerie und Grenzgebiete,* 28, 368-374.

Mayr, E., 1997, The Objects of Selection. *Proceedings of the National Academy of Sciences USA*, 94, 2091-2094.

McClenon, J., 2002, *Wondrous healing, Shamanism, Human Evolution and the Origin of Religion.* Northern Illinois University Press, De Kalb, Ill.

McLeod, K., 2016, *A Trackless Path. A Commentary on the great completion (dzogchen) teaching of Jingmé Lingpa's Revelation of Ever-present Good.* Sonoma, Ca. Unfettered Mind Media.

Miles-Yepez, N., 2006, *The Common Heart, An Experience of Interreligious Dialogue.* New York, Lantern Books.

Miller, S. L. and Urey, H. C., 1959, Organic compound synthesis on the primitive earth. *Science,* 130, 245-251

Moritz, J. M., 2016, *Science and Religion. Beyond warfare and toward understanding.* Winona MN., Anselm Academic.

Murphy, T. R., 2010, The role of religious and mystic experiences in human evolution: A corollary hypothesis for neurotheology. *NeuroQuantology,* 4, 495-508.

Newberg, A.B., 2010, *Principles of Neurotheology.* New York, Routledge.

Nhát Hahn, T., 1991, *Old Path White Clouds. Walking the footsteps of the Buddha.* Berkeley, CA, Parallax Press.

Nhát Hahn, T. and Kapleau, P., 2005, *Zen Keys.* Three Leaves Press.

Nicholson, R. A., 1914, *The Mystics of Islam.* London, Penguin Books.

Noelle, D.C., 2003, Searching for God in the machine. In Kurtz, P. ed. *Science and Religion, are they compatible?* Amherst New York, Prometheus Books, p 313-319.

Pennock, R.T, 1996, Naturalism, Evidence, and Creationism: The case of Phillip Johnson. *Biology and Philosophy,* 11, 543-549.

Pepperberg, I. M., Koepke, A. Livingston, P., Girard, M. and Hartsvield, L.A., 2013, Reasoning by inference: Further studies on exclusion in grey parrots (Psittaus erithacus), *Journal of Comparative Psychology,* 127, 272-281.

Persinger, M. A., 1987, *Neuropsychological bases of God beliefs.* New York, Praeger.

Persinger, M. A. and Healey, F., 2002, Experimental facilitation of the sensed presence: Possible intercalation between the hemispheres induced by complex magnetic fields. *Journal of Nervous and Mental Disease,* 190, 533-541.

Pew Research Center, 2019 *In U.S., Decline of Christianity Continues at Rapid Pace. An update on America's changing religious landscape.* https://www.pewforum. org/2019/10/17/in-u-s-decline-of-christianity-continues-at-rapid-pace.

Plante, T. G., ed., 2010, *Contemplative Practices in Action.* Santa Barbara, CA, Praeger.

Plotkin, H., 2000, People Do More Than Imitate. *Scientific American,* 283, p, 72.

Pope Francis, 2015, *On Care for our Common Home. Laudato si',* Washington, D.C., United States Conference of Catholic Bishops.

Popper, K. R., 1959, *The Logic of Scientific Discovery.* New York, Basic Books.

Prothero, S. *God is Not One. The Eight Rival Religions That Run the World.* New York, HarperOne.

Raichle, M. E., MacLeod, A. M., Snyder, A. Z., Powers, W. J., Gusnard, D. A., Shulman, G. L., 2001, A default mode of brain function. *Proceedings of the National Academy of Science,* 98, 676-682.

Ram Dass, 1971, *Be Here Now.* New York, Crown Publishing Group.

Ram Dass, 2000, *Still Here. Embracing Aging, Changing, and Dying.* New York, Riverhead books.

Roberts, P. (translator), 2011, *Mahamudra and Related Instructions.* Library of Tibetan Classics, Sommerville MA, Wisdom Publications.

Rohr, R., 2003, *Everything Belongs. The Gift of Contemplative Prayer.* New York, Crossroad Publishing Company.

Rohr, R., 2009, *The Naked Now, Learning to See as the Mystics See.* New York, Crossroad Publishing Company.

Salzberg, S., 2002, *Faith. Trusting your own deepest experience,* New York, Riverhead Books.

Savin, J. L., and Rabin, J. 1997, The neural substrates of religious experience. *Journal of Neuropsychiatry,* 9, 498-510.

Schjoedt, U. , 2011, The neural correlates of religious experience. *Religion,* 41, 91-95.

Shapiro, R., 2013, *Perennial Wisdom for the Spiritually Independent. Sacred Teachings – Annotated & Explained.* Woodstock, Vt, Skylight Paths Publishing.

Shapiro, R., 2017, *Holy Rascals. Advice for Spiritual Revolutionaries.* Boulder CO, Sounds True.

Shermer, M., 2011, *The Believing Brain. From ghosts and gods to politics and conspiracies – How we Construct beliefs and reinforce them as truths.* New York. St. Martins Press, 385p.

Shukla, S., Acharya, S., and Rajput, D., 2013, Neurotheology – Matters of the mind of matters that mind? *Journal of Clinical and Diagnostic Research,* 7, 1486-1490.

Siegel, R., Strassfeld, M. and Strassfeld, S., 1973 *The Jewish Catalog: A do-it-yourself kit.* Philadelphia, Jewish publication Society of America.

Smith, H., 1991, *The World's Religions.* New York, HarperCollins.

Smith, H., 2001, *Why Religion Matters.* New York, HarperCollins.

Stark R. and Finke R., 2000, *Acts of faith: Explaining the human side of religion.* Berkeley, University of California Press.

Taylor, A. H., Hunt, G. R., Medina, F.S. and Gray, R.D., 2009, Do New Caledonian crows solve physical problems through causal reasoning? *Proceedings of the Royal Society B,* 276, 247-254.

Taylor, J. B., 2006, *My Stroke of Insight. A Brain Scientist's Personal Journey.* New York, Penguin.

Teasdale, W., 1999, *The Mystic Heart. Discovering a Universal Spirituality in The World's Religions.* Novato, CA, New World Library.

Tedrus, G.M.A.S., Fonseca, L. C., and Höehr, G. C., 2014, Spirituality aspects in patients with epilepsy. *Seizure,* 23, 25-28.

Toga, R.W. and Thompson, 2003, Mapping Brain Asymmetry. *Nature Reviews. Neuroscience,* 4, 37 – 48.

Underhill, E., 1911, *Mysticism. The preeminent study in the nature and development of spiritual consciousness.* New York, Doubleday.

Urgesi, C., Agloti, S.M., Skrap, M., Fabbro, F., 2010, The spiritual brain: Selective cortical lesions Modulate Human self-Transcendence. *Neuron,* 65, 309-319.

Valvo, A. 1972, *Sight Restoration after Long-term Blindness: the Problems and Behavior Patterns of Visual Rehabilitation.* New York, American Foundation for the Blind.

Vligenthart, D., 2011, Can neurotheology explain religion? *Archive for the Psychology of Religion,* 33, 137-171.

Wall, J.T.; Xu, J.; Wang, X. (2002). Human brain plasticity: an emerging view of the multiple substrates and mechanisms that cause cortical changes and related sensory dysfunctions after injuries of sensory inputs from the body. *Brain Research Reviews,* 39, 181–215.

Wilber, K., 1995, *Sex, Ecology, Spirituality, The Spirit of Evolution.* Boston, Shambhala Publication.

Wilber, K., 2006, Forward to Miles-Yepez, N. *The Common Heart, An Experience of Interreligious Dialogue.* New York, Lantern Books.

Wilber, K., 2007, *Integral Spirituality. A Startling New Role for Religion in the Modern and Postmodern World.* Boston, Shambhala Publications.

Williams, P. S., 2013, *C.S. Lewis vs. the New Atheists.* London, Paternoster.

Wilson, D.S., 2002, *Darwin's Cathedral, Evolution, Religion, and the Nature of Society.* Chicago, University of Chicago Press.

Wilson, E.O., 1998, *Consilience. The Unity of Knowledge.* New York, Vintage Books.

Yogananda, P., 1946, *Autobiography of a Yogi.* New York, The Philosophical Library.

Endnotes

1. Major neoatheist authors include Richard Dawkins (2006), Daniel Dennett (2006), Sam Harris (2004), Christopher Hitchens (2007), and E. O. Wilson (1998).

2. Armstrong (2000)

3. Pew Research Center (2019) https://www.pewforum.org/2019/10/17/in-u-s-decline-of-christianity-continues-at-rapid-pace/

4. Shapiro (2013)

5. Pew Research Center (2019) https://www.pewforum.org/2019/10/17/in-u-s-decline-of-christianity-continues-at-rapid-pace/

6. Mind and consciousness are often considered synonyms, but in Buddhism there is a subtle difference. Consciousness is the sensation one gets from one's senses. There is consciousness from sight, sound, touch, taste, smell and in Buddhism there is also a mental consciousness – an awareness of what is going on in one's thoughts. Mind is thus a combination of all these types of consciousness. In this book I will use the term "mind" in this context. In contrast, when I use the term "consciousness" I talk about the mental consciousness, the awareness of what is going on in one's thoughts.

7. There are many other elementary particles, but these are elementary enough for our purposes.

8. I am ignoring neutrons in this discussion. Neutrons may be present in the nucleus of some atoms. The presence of a neutron changes the atomic weight of an element, but it does not change the chemical properties.

9. Dennett (1991)

10. For a discussion of this see Barbour (1997)

11. Shapiro (2013)

12. Teasdale (1999)

13. The Dalai Lama in the forward to the Gyurme Dorje translation of the *Tibetan Book of the Dead* (2006) New York, Penguin Books.
14. Teasdale (1999)
15. Frost (2010)
16. Pepperberg et al. (2013)
17. Taylor et al. (2009)
18. See Bergson (1911)
19. See Miller and Urey (1959). Miller and Urey (1959) assumed that the early atmosphere was more reducing than now is considered reasonable. Modern studies however using a less reducing atmosphere also produced organic molecules, although the yield was lower.
20. http://assets.pewresearch.org/wp-content/uploads/sites/11/2009/12/multiplefaiths.pdf
21. James (1902)
22. Experience of James Russel Lowell as reported by James (1902)
23. The experience of Dr. R. M. Burke as reported by James (1902)
24. Lama Sheng, The Ultimate Supreme Path of Mahamudra in Library of Tibetan Classics (2011) *Mahamudra and Related Instructions*. Translated by Peter Roberts, Sommerville MA, Wisdom Publications. P. 101 – 102.
25. Doyle (1997)
26. Acts 22:6-11, The New Revised Standard Version
27. From Hixon (1992)
28. Quran, Surah 53:4-9
29. Armstrong (2002)
30. Underhill (1911)
31. James (1902)
32. James (1902)
33. Williams (2013)
34. Barbour (1997)
35. Shermer (2011)
36. This is the terminology used by Rohr (2009)
37. See Armstrong (2000) and (2009)
38. Valvo (1972)
39. Matthew 7.1, The New Revised Standard Version
40. Rohr (2009)
41. See Keating (1995), Teasdale, (1999)
42. Teasdale (1999)
43. Salzberg (2002)
44. DeMello (1990)
45. See Hixon (1992)
46. Smith (1991)
47. A good example of this is Prothero (2010)
48. Armstrong (2009)

49. Armstrong (2000)

50. http://assets.pewresearch.org/wp-content/uploads/sites/11/2009/12/multiplefaiths.pdf

51. Rohr (2003)

52. Shapiro (2017)

53. These stages are also called preconventional, conventional, post conventional; or egocentric, ethnocentric, and worldcentric, see Wilber (2007)

54. Wilber (2007)

55. Wilber (2007)

56. Wilber (2007)

57. Wilber (2006)

58. See Smith (2001), Moritz (2016), and Larson and Ruse (2017)

59. Alumkal (2017)

60. See Moritz (2016)

61. Moritz (2016)

62. Popper (1959)

63. Actually radioactive decay relates to isotopes of an element, rather than the element itself. For example ^{235}U (i.e. the isotope of uranium with an atomic weight of 235) decays to ^{207}Pb whereas ^{238}U decays to ^{206}Pb. However, that detail is not important in this discussion.

64. Dawkins (1976)

65. Lipton and Bhaerman (2009)

66. Borgman (1998)

67. Quote from Greenberg, (2000)

68. Kuhn (1962)

69. For more details see Pennock (1996)

70. Ashbrook (1984)

71. Newberg (2010)

72. Toga and Thompson (2003)

73. Newberg (2010)

74. Persinger (1987)

75. Dewhurst and Beard (1970), Savin and Rabin (1997), Tedrus et al. (2014), Arzy and Schurr (2016)

76. Dewhurst and Beard (1970), Devinsky and Lai (2008), Arzy and Schurr (2016)

77. Dewhurst and Beard (1970), Devinsky and Lai (2008)

78. Newberg (2010)

79. Compare Persinger and Healy (2002) with Grandqvist et al., (2005)

80. Persinger (1987)

81. Raichle et al. (2001)

82. Brewer et al. (2011), Goleman and Davidson (2017)

83. Urgesi, et al. (2010)

84. Savin and Rabin (1997)

85. The insula is a portion of the brain that lies between the parietal and temporal lobe.
86. Goleman & Davidson (2017)
87. Azari et al. (2001)
88. Shukla et al. (2013)
89. See Geertz (2009), Goldberg (2009), Murphy (2010), Schjoedt (2011), Vliegenthart (2011), and Shukla et al. (2013)
90. Cunningham (2011)
91. Vliegenthart (2011)
92. See for example Persinger (1987)
93. See for example Cunningham (2011), Schjoedt (2011) and Vliegenthart (2011)
94. Cunningham (2011)
95. Shukla et al. (2013)
96. Wall et al. (2002)
97. Lonton (1979)
98. Davis et al. (1999)
99. Taylor (2006)
100. Taylor (2006)
101. Ram Dass (2000)
102. For example, Newberg (2010), Goleman and Davidson (2017).
103. Goleman and Davidson (2017)
104. Newberg (2010)
105. Barbour (1997)
106. Newberg (2010)
107. See Harris (2004), Dennett (2006), Dawkins (2006), and Hitchens (2007)
108. Persinger (1987)
109. Persinger (1987)
110. Shermer (2011)
111. Shermer (2011)
112. Perhaps the major proponent of this argument is Harris (2004), although Dawkins (2006) also uses it.
113. Harris (2004), see also Dawkins (2006)
114. Persinger (1987)
115. Persinger (1987)
116. Noelle (2003)
117. Freemon (1976)
118. Dewhurst and Beard (1970), Persinger (1987), Savin and Rabin (1997), Devinsky and Lai (2008).
119. Tedrus et al. (2014)
120. Newberg (2010)
121. Frost (2010)
122. Dawkins (2006)

123. Dawkins (2006)

124. Wilson (2002), Shermer (2011)

125. Dawkins (2006)

126. See Dawkins (2006)

127. Persinger (1987)

128. McClenon (2002)

129. Dawkins (2006)

130. Dawkins (1976)

131. Dawkins (2006)

132. Benítez-Bribiesca (2001)

133. Mayr (1997)

134. See for example, Mayr (1997), Boyd and Richardson (2000), and Plotkin (2000)

135. Diamond (1997)

136. Stark and Finke (2000)

137. Nhat Hahn (1991)

138. Huxley (1945)

139. Matthew 6.6 The New Revised Standard Version.

140. Keating (1986)

141. Ferguson (2010)

142. Quoted from Gabriel (1965)

143. Keating (1986)

144. Keating (1994)

145. Keating (1986)

146. Frenette (2011)

147. Inayat Kahn (2010)

148. Campbell (1962)

149. McLeod (2016)

150. Good examples of this attitude are given by Bachelor (1997) and Harris (2014).

151. Chopra and Simon (2004)

152. Armstrong (2019)

153. Keating (1994)

154. Armstrong (2019)

155. Cited from Armstrong (2019)

156. Huxley (1945)

157. Nicholson (1914)

158. Kavanaugh and Rodriguez (1980)

159. Nhát Hahn and Kapleau (2005)

160. https://www.thebalance.com/income-inequality-in-america-3306190

161. https://www.cdc.gov/nchs/products/databriefs/db328.htm

162. Pope Francis (2015)

163. For example, see Wilber (1995) or Rohr (2003)

164. Wilber (1995)

165. Rohr (2003)

166. Fields (1992)

167. Goldberg (2010)

168. Goldberg (2010)

169. Fields (1992)

170. https://www.theosophical.org

171. Goldberg (2010)

172. Frenette (2011)

173. Contemplative Outreach website:
     https://www.contemplativeoutreach.org/history-contemplative-outreach

174. Siegel et al. (1973)

175. As documented by Kamenetz (1994)

176. Kamenetz (1994)

177. Inayat-Kahn (2011)

178. Hermansen (1997)

179. Summarized from Inayat-Kahn (2011)

180. Thomas Keating in Miles-Yepez (2006)

181. From Kamenetz (1994)

182. Teasdale (1999)

183. Miles-Yepez (2006)

184. See summaries in Plante (2010) and Bush (2011)

185. For details see Cullen (2011)

186. https://www.sciencealert.com/
     yoga-and-meditation-in-the-us-are-totally-exploding-right-now

187. https://www.yogauonline.com/yoga-news/
     yoga-journal-study-20-million-americans-practice-yoga

188. https://www.behavioralessentials.com/
     the-benefits-of-mindfulness-in-the-workplace/

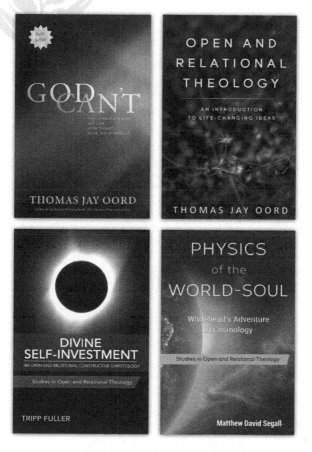

Made in the USA
Middletown, DE
30 March 2022

63241534R10129